Biblical Truth About Difficult Concepts

Don T. Phillips

"Biblical Truths About Difficult Concepts," by Don T. Phillips. ISBN 978-1-63868-108-3.

Published 2023 by Virtualbookworm.com Publishing Inc., P.O. Box 9949, College Station, TX 77845, US. Copyright ©2023 Don T. Phillips.

All rights reserved. No part of this publication may be reproduced, stored in a retrieval system, or transmitted in any form or by any means, electronic, mechanical, recording or otherwise, without the prior written permission of Don T. Phillips.

Dedication

This book is dedicated to:

Philip Blackburn

And

Weldon Mackey

Christian Brothers

and

Real Men

Preface

The Holy Bible is a magnificent manuscript which was written over a span of 1500 years by at least 40 different authors. Most Bible scholars believe that the *Book of Job* was the first book of the Bible to be written. Almost all Christians regardless of denomination believe that the Holy Scriptures were written by ordinary men with extraordinary inspiration under the influence of the Holy Spirit. Everything that man needs to know about God and everything that is needed to find eternal life in His only Son, Jesus Christ, is written in this manuscript between the Book of Genesis which begins the Old Testament and the Book of Revelation which ends the New Testament. All born-again Christians believe that the Bible is God inspired:

All scripture is given by inspiration of God, and is profitable for doctrine, for reproof, for correction, for instruction in righteousness II Timothy 3:16

It has been estimated that over 85 % of the houses in America have some version of the Holy Bible. Although any true Christian believer will assert that the Bible is a book of truth which is God -inspired, not all people hold that belief. However, scholarly investigations have estimated that only between 25% and 35% of all Christians believe that the bible is literally true. This present Age has been shrinking. Part of this movement may be because when one believes that the Holy Bible is inerrant truth, this should only apply to the original Hebrew/Aramaic and Greek manuscripts which were originally penned. As far as English versions are concerned, the first complete English Language version of the Bible probably dates from 1382 and was credited to John Wycliffe and his followers. The first complete English Bible translated directly from the Hebrew and Greek is usually attributed to William Tyndale around 1526 AD. He was executed by King Henry VIII for daring to produce a Bible that common people could read, undermining the power of the clergy. The King James Bible was published in 1611. It remains the most widely published text in the English Language, and was the work of around 50 scholars who were appointed in 1604 by King James.

Many people have abandoned the King James Bible claiming that it is *too hard to read*; *out of date*; *no longer appropriate for modern Christians*, etc……. There are now over 50 versions of the Bible in print today and more being published every decade. Several modern versions promote the work of Satan to institutionalize the Holy Word of God and justify sinful behavior. There have been attempts to remove or change verses which do not support modern cultural behavior or perverted behavior. Every Christian should reject all modern versions which radically change the original word of God. The Authorized King James Version stood for over 400 years as a primary source of truth and accuracy, and it will be used in this manuscript. This book will support all conclusions based upon the King James Bible. Regardless of which version of the Holy Bible might be used in any one church, organization or personal study…. one thing has remained practically unchanged.

[16] For God so loved the world, that he gave his only begotten Son, that whosoever believeth in him should not perish, but have everlasting life.
[17] For God sent not his Son into the world to condemn the world; but that the world through him might be saved   John 3 :16-17

For by grace are ye saved through faith; and that not of yourselves: it is the gift of God   Ephesians 2:8

In addition to deliberately changing the original Greek and Hebrew manuscripts, modern misunderstanding and denominational beliefs have evolved which are simply wrong. This is not only Spiritually damaging, but is completely against the original intent of God. In the Old Testament, God established only one religion called *Judaism*. There were only two classes of people: *Jews* and *Gentiles*. When Christ came and died on the Cross of Calvary, He replaced salvation by works under the Old Covenant (Jews) with a new and better religious system based upon faith and grace (Jews and Gentiles). This new system was called *Christianity*, and the people who became known as *Christians* were intended to be a unified and homogeneous group of people who would accept Jesus Christ as their Lord and Savior. There was to be only one religious structure in which all Christians would worship.

One Lord, one faith, one baptism   Ephesians 4:5

Let your conversation be as it becometh the gospel of Christ: that whether I come and see you, or else be absent, I may hear of your affairs, that ye stand fast in one Spirit, with one mind striving together for the faith of the gospel
Philippians 1:27

These two verses from the Apostle Paul show that Christianity is more about a unified and common relationship with the Living God rather than a set of rules or ordinances. It is from this guiding principle that a common religious system should have emerged. There was never any intent to establish the wide variety of religious systems which exist today. Common beliefs and common Christian principles have fractured Biblical Truth so badly that some denominations will preach that if a Christian is not baptized a certain way, it is a sin: other denominations teach that if you are not a member of their denomination that you will go to hell: Others teach that if one does not tithe 10%, he/she is committing a sin against God: Still others teach that if you do not confess your sins to appointed clergy that you will die in sin.

How sad that Christ died upon the Cross of Calvary to redeem all men from sin. He is *the way, the truth and the life*. Salvation is now based upon faith and grace......not by baptism, tithing, confessions of sin or any other religious practice. There are many today that preach salvation can be obtained by faith plus nothing....and they are right.

This book was written to establish truth; not truth based upon the beliefs of man but on the Word of God. Jesus Christ declared during His earthly ministry of reconciliation that:

Jesus saith unto him, I am the way, the truth, and the life: no man cometh unto the Father, but by me   John 14:6

[9] *For we are laborers together with God: ye are God's husbandry, ye are God's building.*
[10] *According to the grace of God which is given unto me, as a wise master-builder, I have laid the foundation, and another builds thereon. But let every man take heed how he builds thereupon.*
[11] *For other foundation can no man lay than that is laid, which is Jesus Christ*
I Corinthians 3: 9-11

This book was written to urge all Christians to seek the truth, and challenge those requirements of basic principles and practices that organized religion teaches with what is truth from the Holy Word of God. There are 6 basic religious principles which have been examined.

Chapter 1: *The Dispensational Structure of the Holy Bible*

It is impossible to understand the New Covenant without a complete understanding of Dispensational Truth. A *dispensation* is simply a period of time during which God has dealt with His creation in a particular way. Except for basic, fundamental principles, one cannot apply the commands and rules that God gave to man in one dispensation and apply them to another.

Chapter 2: *Baptism*

Baptism is one of the least understood and misinterpreted Christian practices in modern religion. It will be shown that baptism is not necessary for salvation and never has been.

Chapter 3: *Tithing*

Tithing was a requirement by God under Old Testament Law, but it was never intended to be a commandment of God under the New Covenant. It will be shown that a required 10% tithe under the New Covenant of faith and grace is a myth of clergy and seminaries.

Chapter 4: *The Role of the Holy Spirit Under the New Covenant*

The power and role of the Holy Spirit is almost completely misunderstood by ordinary Christians. The Holy Spirit is sent to all born-again believers and it is through the Holy Spirit that all true-believers are baptized into the body of Christ. Jesus promised to send the Holy Spirit to dwell in every born-again believer, and function as a permanent guide, teacher, seal of salvation, and comforter for all true believers (John 14:16-18). He also promised that the Holy Spirit's power would help His followers defeat Satan and spread the message of the gospel around the world:

Chapter 5: *The Genealogy of Jesus Christ*

God sent his only Son…. Jesus Christ……to a sinful world to reconcile all men to Himself and to redeem them from all sin……*past*, *present* and *future*. Jesus Christ was uniquely qualified to be the Savior of the world and live a sinless life under the Law. The genealogy of Jesus Christ proves that He was a direct descendent of Abraham and a direct descendent of King David. He was qualified and born to be our Great High Priest and eternal King.

This Chapter will compare the genealogy in the Gospel pf Matthew to that contained in the gospel of Luke, and discuss why they are different.

Chapter 6: *Life After Death*

The vast majority of Christians do not understand what will happen to the body, soul, and Spirit of man upon physical death. The common teaching that one will be ascend to Heaven upon death, but this belief cannot be sustained by the Holy scriptures and is just not true. This Chapter will reveal what will happen to all men (believers and unbelievers) upon death. The biblical truth might surprise you!

Chapter 7: The Seven Feasts of Israel

Within the Old Testament Book of Leviticus, God has provided a blueprint for the 1st and 2nd coming of Jesus Christ. This blueprint is the *7 Holy Feasts of Israel*. The 1st four feasts (Passover, Unleavened Bread, Firstfruits and Pentecost) were all fulfilled in shadow and type at the 1st advent of Jesus Christ, and all take place in the Spring of the year. The last three feasts (Trumpets, Yom Kippur and Tabernacles) will all take place in the Fall, and each will play a major role as the Church age draws to a close. The last 3 Feasts will be fulfilled at the 2nd Coming of Jesus Christ. The 7 Feasts are to be observed each year by the Jews to commemorate and remember how the Nation of Israel was freed by God after serving over 200 years as Egyptian slaves. However, each of the 7 Festivals are also a *Moed*, or a *rehearsal* of things to come. The 1st four Feasts are a rehearsal of the 1st coming of Christ, and the last 3 feasts are a rehearsal of the 2nd coming of Christ. This fascinating and prophetic study will discuss the physical and spiritual application of each Feast. Understanding the *Seven Feasts of Israel* is the key to understanding the Book of Revelation.

In conclusion, this book was written for all New Covenant believers to understand and receive the truth of 6 important New Covenant practices. It was basically written to free Christians from the *Curse of the Law* and to understand God's Holy Word. *Maranatha* and may God Bless you abundantly.

Table of Contents

Dedication i
Preface ii
Table of Contents viii
Chapter 1: The Holy Bible is a Dispensational Manuscript from God 1
Chapter 2: Baptism 12
Chapter 3: Tithing 37
Chapter 4: The Holy Spirit 50
Chapter 5: The Genealogy of Jesus Christ: Matthew and Luke 64
Chapter 6: What Will Happen After Death 70
Chapter 7: The Seven Feasts of Israel 94
BIBLIOGRAPHY 124

Chapter 1

The Holy Bible is a Dispensational Manuscript from God

One cannot possibly understand the Holy Bible without first understanding that the Holy Bible is a *Dispensational Document.* It is God-inspired and God-breathed word, written by prophets of old and by those who He chose to record His words.

All scripture is given by inspiration of God, and is profitable for doctrine, for reproof, for correction, for instruction in righteousness (II Timothy 3:16).

The Holy bible is composed of 66 different Books: 39 in the Old

Testament and 27 in the New Testament. There are 1189 chapters and 31,102 verses. Books of the Bible can be grouped into 9 different categories. The Holy Bible can also be divided into 7 different *dispensations* from Adam and Eve in the Garden of Eden through the 1000-year Millennial Kingdom. A dispensation is simply a period of time during which God is dealing with His people in a new and unique way.

The books of the Bible and their divisions by chapters and verses were arranged by man, but the contents of each book are divinely inspired by God. The original Old Testament was primarily written in Hebrew, with some sections in Aramaic. The New Testament was written in Greek. Chapters, paragraphs and punctuation marks were added to the English version (AKJV). We have shown how the Old and New Testaments were grouped into 9 major categories: 4 groups which compose the *Old Testament* and 5 groups which compose the *New Testament*.

Over the past 200 years biblical scholars have recognized and that the Holy Bible is a historical and religious record which was written as an integrated and unified document describing 7 different and consecutive periods of time during which God has dealt with His creation in separate, unique ways. Each of these 7 periods of time is called a *Dispensation* of time.

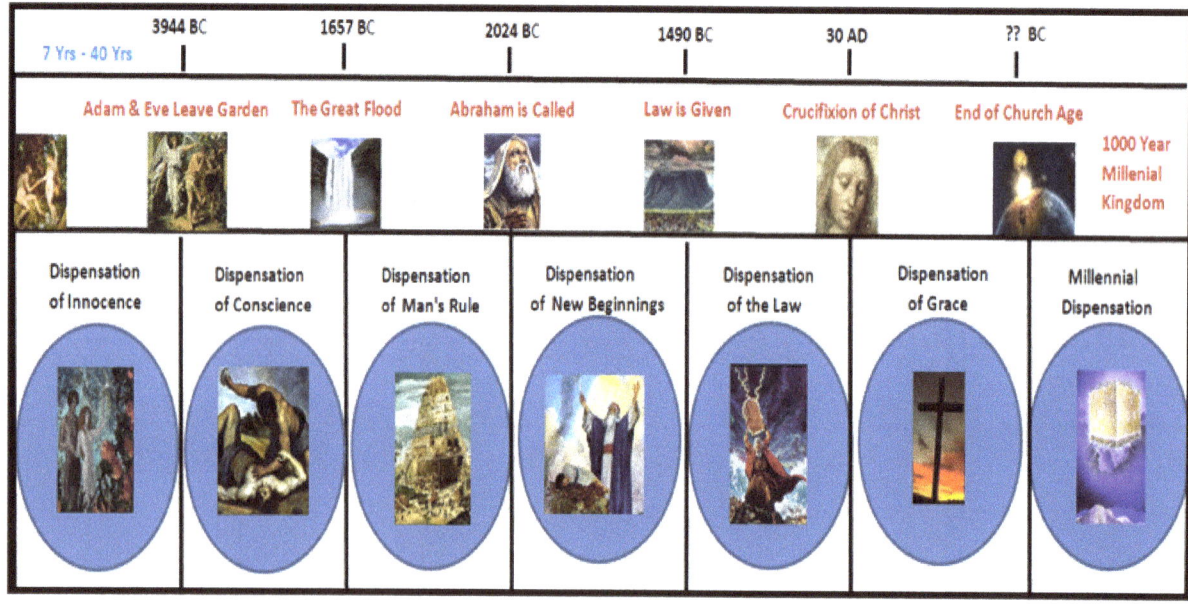

There are 7 different dispensations which are, sequential and non-overlapping, but not equal in length. (1) *The Dispensation of Innocence*…. Genesis 1:1-Genesis 3:7 (2) *The Dispensation of Conscience* …...Genesis 3:8- Genesis 8:22 (3) *The Dispensation of Human Government*…...Genesis 9:1-Genesis 11:32 (4) The

Dispensation of Promise…...Genesis 12:1-Exodus 19:25 (5) The *Dispensation of the Law*…...Exodus 21-Acts 2:4 (6) The Dispensation of Grace…. Acts 2:4-Revelation 20:3 and (7) The *Dispensation of the Millennial Kingdom*…. Revelation 20:3-Revelation 20:6.

This book will not describe and fully explain the first 4 Dispensations nor the seventh. We will only be concerned with the last 3 Dispensations, primarily Dispensations 5 and 6. The Church Age (# 6) which we are in today called the *Dispensation of Grace*: the previous dispensation called the *Age of the Law* (#5): and the last dispensation (#7) called the Millennial Kingdom. If a detailed description of each dispensation is of interest, see: Larkin: *Dispensational Truth*, Phillips: *The Eternal Plan of God* or Ryrie: *Dispensationalism*.

Paul wrote in II Timothy:

Study to shew thyself approved unto God, a workman that need not to be ashamed, rightly dividing the word of truth   II Timothy 2:15

What did Paul mean when he wrote that as New Covenant Christians, we should *rightly divide the word of truth* (The Holy Scriptures). It is not realistic to believe that we should be able to quote each Verse in the Bible, but it is expected that every Christian should be able to distinguish one dispensation in the Bible from another, and to understand why there are 7 dispensations in the Holy Bible. One cannot take what God commanded to his people in one dispensation, and apply it to another. A good example are the dietary rules that God commanded of His people in different dispensations. God told Adam and Eve that they could eat of any fruit in the Garden of Eden except for the fruit of the *Tree of Knowledge* (Adam and Eve were vegetarians). This was in the *Dispensation of Innocence* (#1). When God expunged Adam and Eve from the Garden of Eden, He told them that they could eat meat from the animals of the earth but they could not eat the blood. This was in the *Dispensation of Conscience* (#2). When God gave the Law to Israel through Moses, He included dietary restrictions. For example, they could not eat any animal with a cloven hoof who chews its cud, and could not eat a variety of seafood. This was in the *Dispensation of the Law* (#5).

When Jesus Christ died upon the Cross of Calvary, He set every Jew and every Gentile free from the curse of the Law. Peter was sent to preach salvation by *Faith* and *Grace* to the Jews and the apostle Paul was sent to the Gentiles. One day Peter was asked to sit and eat with a group of Gentiles, but he declared that he would never eat with a Gentile because such it was forbidden under the law. Peter said: *I have never eaten anything that is common or unclean* (Acts 10:14). God quickly corrected Peter, and told Him that: *What God hath cleansed, call not thou common* (Acts 10:15). This is an example that any child can understand. And confirms that what God commanded of man in one dispensation cannot be applied to another dispensation. Another example is a command that God gave Abraham concerning male circumcism. When Abraham was 99 years old, God appeared to him and instructed him to circumcise himself and all male members of his household. God ordained *Circumcision* as an everlasting sign between Him and Abraham of His unconditional, covenant promises to Abraham and his seed (Genesis 17: 9-10). Circumcism was ordained by God in the Dispensation of New Beginnings was *before* the *Dispensation of the Law*, but the act of circumcision was a sign and continued as a command through the Dispensation of the Law. This commandment was rendered non-binding during the *Dispensation of Grace*, but is still being observed by Jews today. This was to be a sign of God's unilateral covenant with Abraham that his offspring (seed) would be blessed and that they would live in the Land of Canaan forever (Genesis 17: 10-11). The first requirement God imposed on Israel was obedience: *if you obey my voice*. Obedience to God's voice would be the test by which Israel would demonstrate to the world that it trusted in God and that it would live according to God's words. The second requirement was that Israel *obey the laws of the covenant*: *if you keep my covenant*…. The demands of the covenant were the laws and statutes that regulated the relationship between Israel and God and the laws and statutes that regulated life under the Old Covenant. However, under the New Covenant the apostle Paul emphatically stated that circumcism was not necessary to obtain salvation (Romans 2: 25-29). This seems to be in direct conflict with Genesis 17:10. There is no conflict once God's covenant relationship with Abraham is understood.

There are two types of covenants between God and man: *conditional* and *unconditional*. A conditional covenant is based upon a covenant between two parties and is valid as long as each party does not violate the agreement (s). Once violated, the covenant promise is null and void. An unconditional covenant is valid as long as the covenant is in force, regardless of whether one or both parties fail to live up to the stated conditions. The Abrahamic covenant was an unconditional covenant between God and Abraham which was eternal. The *Abrahamic Covenant* included the following promises by God to Abraham and his offspring.

(1) God would bless and multiply the descendants (seed) of Abraham
(2) Abraham would be the father of many nations and Kings

> (3) The descendants of Abraham would one day inherit and live on the entire Land of Canaan

These were unconditional promises that God made unilaterally to Abraham and his seed. Recall that God established these things with Abraham by causing him to fall into a deep sleep, and then he slaughtered animals…. placed them parallel in a row…and then passed between them as Abraham slept. This covenant was ratified by *blood*. God swore that these things would come to pass with himself as a witness, since there could be no higher authority than God Himself. There were two promises to Abraham and his progeny that sealed this agreement: (1) All male descendants of Abraham's seed had to be circumcised and (2) His wife's name would be changed from Sari to Sarah (Genesis 17: 10-15). *Sari* means *princess* in Hebrew and *Sarah* means *princess of the multitude*. From that time on, circumcism was a sign of the unilateral promises which God made to Abraham. it was to be a sign *forever* (Genesis 17: 13-14). Now the paradox: The apostle Paul clearly stated that:

[3] *For I testify again to every man that is circumcised, that he is a debtor to do the whole law.*
[4] *Christ is become of no effect unto you, whosoever of you are justified by the law; ye are fallen from grace.*
[5] *For we through the Spirit wait for the hope of righteousness by faith.*
[6] *For in Jesus Christ neither circumcision avails anything, nor uncircumcision; but faith which worketh by love*   Galatians 5: 3-6

Paul was a Jew who knew the difference between living under the Law and living under faith and grace. He declared that anyone who practiced circumcism was living under the law and not under grace. Paul is correct to say that Christ cancelled the bondage of the law…...every New Covenant member of the body of Christ is not under the law. The promise which God made to Abraham is eternally valid because God had unconditionally promised that the descendants of Abraham would be blessed and inherit the land. God cannot disallow His promises, and even if Israel apostatizes and fails to follow the commandments of God…. including circumcism. Israel will one day possess all of the Land of Canaan. We know that this will not happen until the Church Age is over and the Millennial Kingdom begins.

[22] *Therefore say unto the house of Israel, Thus saith the Lord GOD;* ***I do not this for your sakes, O house of Israel, but for mine Holy name's sake****, which ye have*

profaned among the heathen, whither ye went.

[23] And I will sanctify my great name, which was profaned among the heathen, which ye have profaned in the midst of them; and the heathen shall know that I am the LORD, saith the Lord GOD, when I shall be sanctified in you before their eyes.

[24] *For I will take you from among the heathen, and gather you out of all countries, and will bring you into your own land.*

[25] Then will I sprinkle clean water upon you, and ye shall be clean: from all your filthiness, and from all your idols, will I cleanse you.

[26] A new heart also will I give you, and a new Spirit will I put within you: and I will take away the stony heart out of your flesh, and I will give you an heart of flesh.

[27] And I will put my Spirit within you, and cause you to walk in my statutes, and ye shall keep my judgments, and do them.

*[28] **And ye shall dwell in the land that I gave to your fathers**; and ye shall be my people, and I will be your God*   Ezekiel 36: 22-28

God cannot lie and he will give the Land of Canaan to the Jews as He had promised. However, circumcism is not required to inherit the land, it is only a sign between man and God that this will one day happen. Make no mistake about it, any Jew who will inherit the land must be saved by faith and grace to receive the promises. The Jews are the chosen people of God and they will live in the land. The Gentiles were only saved under the New Covenant, and they will serve Jesus Christ. One has a heavenly calling and one has an earthly calling, but both are saved by faith and grace.

Although it is important to distinguish one dispensation from another. We will only provide details on two: (1) *The Dispensation of the Law* and (2) *The Dispensation of Grace*. The diagram on the next page will frame our discussion.

The *Dispensation of the Law* was initiated at Mt. Sinai after Moses had led the Children of Israel through the Red Sea. Most Christians define the *law* as the 10 Commandments, but there were actually 113 different commandments given to Israel by God to govern their social, religious and political life. These commandments (covenant) were *conditional*. God told the people that if *they would follow His commands that they would be blessed, and that if they disobeyed, they would be cursed.* His covenant promises to Abraham were unconditional.

King David unified the people after years of disobedience, and his son Solomon replaced the Tabernacle with a permanent temple in Jerusalem. The unified

Kingdom of King David and King Solomon split into two parts after the death of Solomon.: The Northern Kingdom which was called *Israel* and the Southern Kingdom which was called *Judah*. Sadly, both apostatized, engaged in idol worship and both were taken into captivity: The Northern Kingdom by *Assyria* and later the Southern Kingdom by *Babylon*. The northern 10 tribes of Israel vanished into history, but the southern Kingdom was preserved by God. After 70 years of Babylonian captivity, they were allowed to return home. The Southern Kingdom of Judah was punished by God for 70 years for failing to observe 70 Sabbatical years of rest for the land over a period of 490 years. Judah was restored by God to preserve the line of King David and eventually ensure that Jesus Christ would arise out of the Kingdom of Judah. Israel eventually rebelled against God again, and went through a 400-year period during which there were: *no Prophets in the Land*. This is called the *Intertestimal Period* and not much is known about what happened except in the writings of the Jewish rabbis.

The New Covenant

In about 26 AD, John the Baptizer was baptizing Jews to *repentance* in the River Jordan (Mark 1:4).

He said, I am the voice of one crying in the wilderness: Make straight the way of the Lord, as said the prophet Elijah   John 12:3

John the Baptist was called to announce that the long-awaited Jewish Messiah (Jesus Christ) was about to appear. As he Baptized to repentance (not salvation), he looked up and saw Jesus coming down the road.

*[29] The next day John saw Jesus coming unto him, and saith, Behold the **Lamb of God**, which taketh away the sin of the world.*
[30] This is he of whom I said: After me cometh a man which is preferred before me: for he was before me.
[31] And I knew him not: but that he should be made manifest to Israel, therefore am I come baptizing with water   John 29:31

The time had come for Jesus Christ to redeem all Israel and forgive the sins of Jews and Gentiles alike. However, Jesus would spend all 3.5 years of His ministry speaking to the Jews first. In Romans 1:16 Paul wrote: *I am not ashamed of the gospel, because it is the power of God that brings salvation to everyone who believes:* **First to the Jew, then to the Gentile**. Salvation by faith and grace is intended for all people, but, chronologically, the gospel message was first revealed to the Jewish people before it was revealed to the Gentiles (non-Jewish people).

Jesus preached and taught among the Jews during all 3.5 years of His ministry of reconciliation. At the end of those 3.5 years, he would die a sacrificial death upon the Cross of Calvary and initiate the New Covenant, which would offer salvation to Jews and Gentiles alike by faith and grace…. not by the works of the law. Before the apostle Paul was chosen to reveal the *mystery* of the Church Age the New Covenant was completely unknown to the Jews, Gentiles and Israel (Colossians 1: 26-27). Even after Jesus Christ sacrificed Himself for our sins and ratified the New Covenant, salvation would first be offered to the Jews. This came on the *Day of Pentecost* when the Holy Spirit fell upon Jews from all over the known world who had gathered in Jerusalem to observe the *Feast of Pentecost*. After offering salvation by faith and grace to the Jews, the corporate body of Jews, Sadducees and Pharisees would stone Steven as he preached the New Gospel of Jesus Christ (Acts 7-8). After this final act of corporate rejection, God turned his face away from the Jews and reached out to the Gentiles (Romans 11:25). He chose Paul on the way to Damascus to preach to the Gentiles. Paul became the voice of God to continue to offer the New Covenant to the Gentiles, just as Moses had been chosen to initiate the Old Covenant to the Jews. Paul wrote 13 epistles to the Gentiles, established how the New Covenant had been ratified by Christ, and how the new body of Christ should lead a life in Jesus Christ. We will see in Chapter 4 how the Holy Spirit was sent by Christ to every born-again Christian, and that by the Holy Spirit everyone who believes in faith will be baptized into the Body of Christ.

When the Jews and their political leaders rejected Jesus Christ as their long-awaited Messiah, God turned to the Gentiles to establish His church and build the Body of Christ. However, God had not abandoned the Jews which is taught by certain theologians as *replacement theology*.

[25] For I would not, brethren, that ye should be ignorant of this mystery, lest ye should be wise in your own conceits; that blindness in part is happened to Israel, until the fulness of the Gentiles be come in.
[26] And so all Israel shall be saved: as it is written, There shall come out of Sion the Deliverer, and shall turn away ungodliness from Jacob:
*[27] For this is my **covenant** unto them, when I shall take away their sins*
Romans 11: 25-27

*Now to him that is of power to stablish you according to my gospel, and the preaching of Jesus Christ, according to the revelation of the **mystery**, which was kept secret since the world began*   Romans 16:25

*This is a great **mystery**: but I speak concerning Christ and the church*
Ephesians 5:32

The entire Church Age and the Dispensation of Grace was completely hidden from the Old Testament Prophets and the Jews since time began. God purposed in His heart that this would be a *mystery* by which Jews and Gentiles alike would be saved until it was revealed by the Apostle Paul. Salvation would now be offered to Jews and Gentiles alike, not by the Law but by Faith and Grace. Although corporately the Jews would be blinded in part to the New Covenant, there would be a remnant who would accept Jesus Christ as the son of God and be saved. This remnant was called the *little flock* in Luke 12:32. The blinding of the Jews in part when God turned to the Gentiles to build His church, is why the following graphic shows no portion of the future to the Jews between when Jesus Christ ended the Dispensation of the Law and began the Dispensation of Grace.

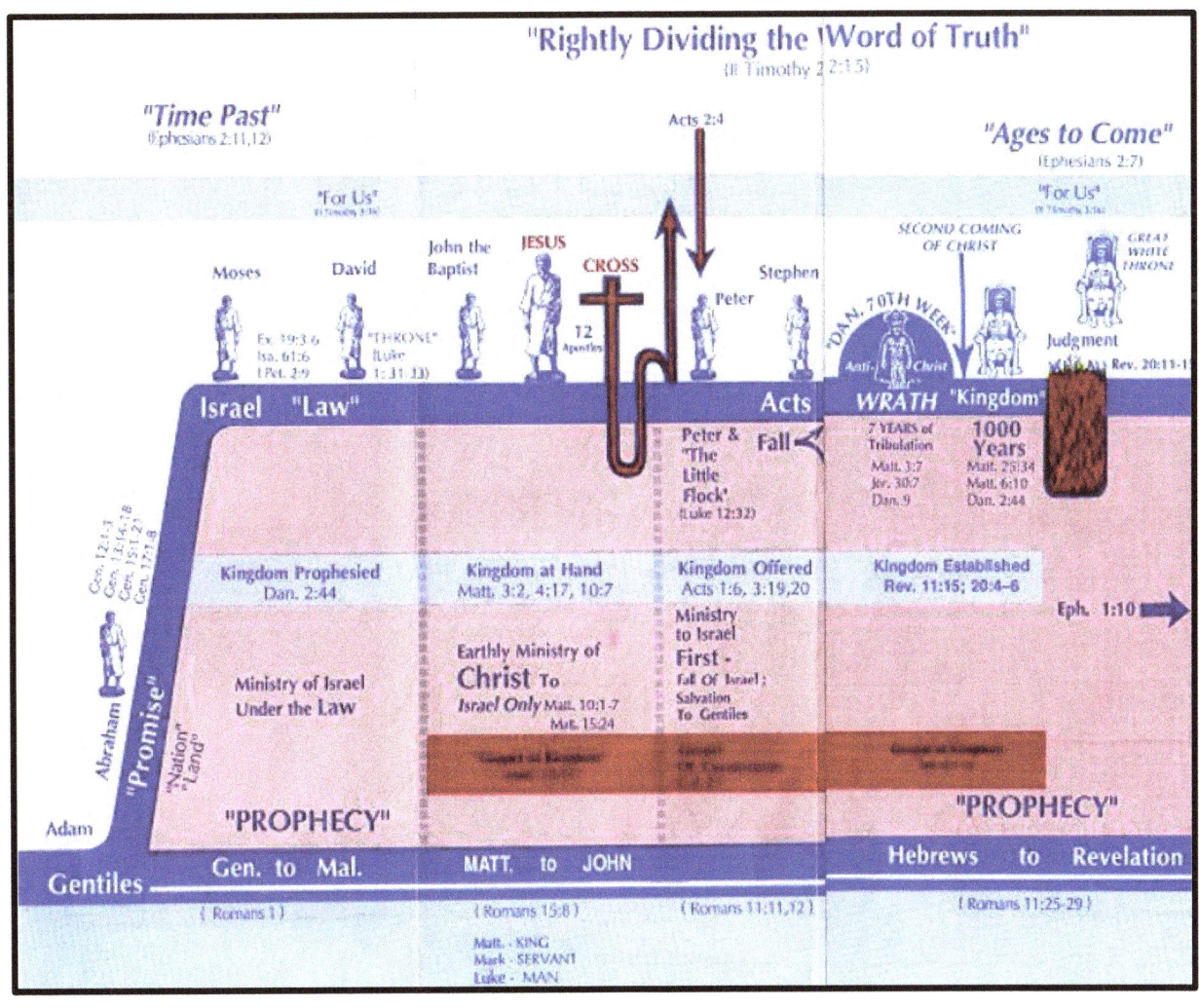

It is precisely this truth which causes a *gap* in the 70th week of Daniel (Daniel 9: 24-27) ......See Phillips, *The Daniel 70 Week Prophecy*. God will not resume His attention to the Nation of Israel until the *Great Tribulation* described by John begins. Note from Revelation 11,12 and 13 that there will be a 3.5-year period of time (Revelation 12:17 Revelation 12:14, Revelation 13:5 and Revelation 11:3) during which Satan will be confined to this earth. After Satan is cast out of heaven by Michael and His Holy angels (Revelation 12: 7-8) Satan will be furious, and He will attempt to destroy Jerusalem, the Jews and the saints (Revelation 12:17). This is the time of *Great Tribulation* which was prophesied by Jesus Christ (Matthew 24-25) and the Old Testament prophets. As far as Israel is concerned, the Church Age simply did not exist. When Satan, the False Prophet and the Antichrist arise during the last 3.5 years of Daniel's 70th week, the Jews will finally realize that Jesus Christ is their hope and their redeemer.

[25] *For I would not, brethren, that ye should be ignorant of this mystery, lest ye should be wise in your own conceits; that* **blindness in part is happened to Israel, until the fulness of the Gentiles be come in.**
[26] *And so all Israel shall be saved: as it is written: There shall come out of Sion the Deliverer, and shall turn away ungodliness from Jacob:*
[27] *For this is my covenant unto them, when I shall take away their sins*
Romans 11: 25-27

A believing remnant from Israel will finally inherit the Land of Canaan during the 1000-year Millennial Kingdom just as God unilaterally promised to Israel. *What about the Church Age*, which is completely hidden from Israel and was a *mystery* until Paul revealed to Jews and Gentiles alike.

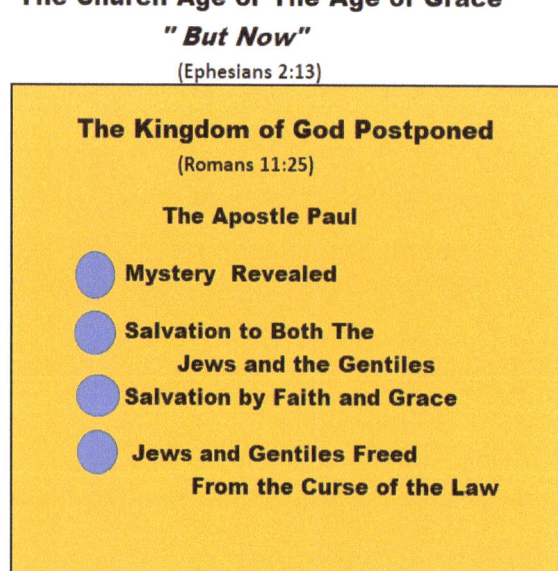

Once again, it must be clearly understood that the Church Age was completely unknown to both the Jews and the Old Testament prophets until the apostle Paul was chosen by God to reveal this *Mystery* (Colossians 1:26). The *Dispensation of Grace* replaced the *Dispensation of the Law*. The entire content of Matthew, Mark Luke and John were a written record of the 3.5-year Ministry of Christ which was *only to the Jews (*Matthew 10:5). Jesus Christ was born a Jew, lived as a Jew and died as Jew.

Without *rightly dividing the Word of Truth*, one cannot possibly completely understand the Church Age and the Age of Grace. Without *rightly dividing the scriptures*, it is also impossible to know the truth concerning Baptism and Tithing in the Church Age. This is the subject of Chapter 2 (Tithing) and Chapter 3 (Baptism).

For the law was given by Moses, but grace and truth came by Jesus Christ John 1:17

And ye shall know the truth, and the truth shall make you free   John 8:32

All scripture is given by inspiration of God, and is profitable for doctrine, for reproof, for correction, for instruction in righteousness   II Timothy 3:16

Chapter 2

Baptism

Introduction

The ordinance of baptism in a New Covenant church is an important concept to understand. If the objective of any New Testament scholar is to stir up a passionate and divisive discussion in almost any church today, this is the place to start. Ecumenical unity base upon a common understanding of baptism is impossible, since each denominational organization will adamantly defend their method and motive for water baptism. Some insist that one must be baptized by total submersion in water; some by sprinkling of water; and some by pouring of water over a believer's head. Some will avoid any controversy by leaving the decision up the person being baptized. This is not only a senseless division of unity, but water baptism is held to be one of two ordinances commanded by Jesus Christ...*Baptism* and *Holy Communion*. God never intended this to happen: There was to be one church (body of Christ), one faith and one gospel. Christ taught unity in the body of Christ and in the beginning, there was nothing but small groups of believers seeking the truth in church doctrine and unity in Jesus Christ. John said it well.

[21] *That they all may be one; as thou, Father, art in me, and I in thee, that they also may be one in us: that the world may believe that thou hast sent me.*
[22] *And the glory which thou gave to me I have given to them; that they may be one, even as we are one:*
[23] *I in them, and thou in me, that they may be made perfect in one; and that the world may know that thou hast sent me, and hast loved them, as thou hast loved me*
John 17: 21-23

In the ecumenical world of today an individual will define his/her Christian belief by the church which is attended. Some denominations will even declare that if one is not a member of that particular denomination, then that person is going to hell. The sacrament of baptism is one of those things that define Spiritual life or death, and not allegiance and belief in our Lord Jesus Christ. Lines have been drawn in the sand, so who is right and who is wrong? There is only one authoritative and absolute source of truth.... and it is the *Holy word of God*. This Chapter will review what has been written and what God has commanded us to do (Ephesians 4:5). The key question is not necessarily *how* one should be baptized but *when….*and is it *required* to find eternal life in Jesus Christ? The result might surprise you.

Old Testament Baptism

The Old Testament is a written record of how God has dealt with man from his creation in the Garden of Eden until the Old Covenant was replaced by the New Covenant. There are 5 different dispensations which have come and gone over this period of time: (1) The Dispensation of Innocence (2) The Dispensation of Conscience (3) The Dispensation of Man's Rule and the (5) Dispensation of the Law.

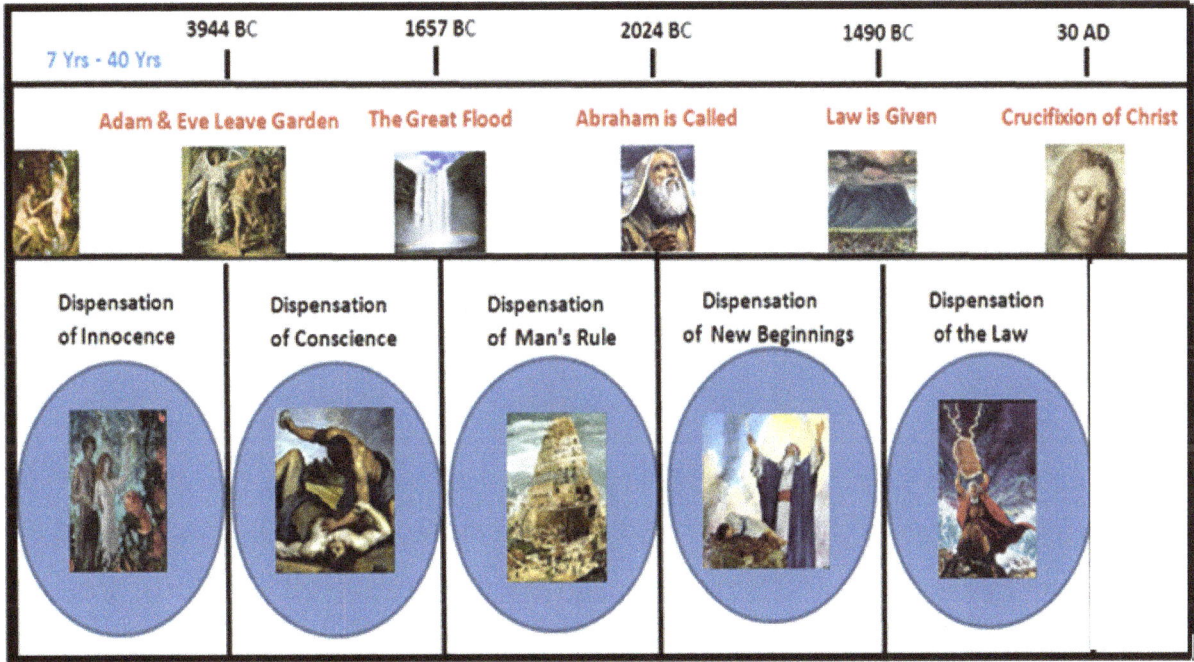

The first mention of water baptism in the Old Testament is often connected to when Noah and his entire family were saved by water. It does not specifically occur in the Old Testament record of the great flood, but was used by Peter (I Peter 3:20-21) while speaking to a group of Jews that had turned to Jesus Christ as their Lord and savior. They were well aware of water baptism and what it meant to every Jew (this will be discussed in some detail later). His remarks are as follows:

[20] *…….. when once the longsuffering of God waited in the days of Noah, while the ark was being prepared, wherein few, that is, eight souls were saved by water.* **[21]** *The like figure whereunto even baptism doth also now save us (not the putting away of the filth of the flesh, but the answer of a good conscience toward God,) by the resurrection of Jesus Christ:*   I Peter 3: 20b-21

Peter declares that *eight souls were saved by water* as a type of *baptism which does now save us*. What is Peter saying? First, it was not the water which saved Noah and his family but it was the Ark. Noah and his family of 8 were safely sealed into the ark, which was a type of all New Covenant believers which are now sealed in Jesus Christ by the Holy Spirit. Jesus Christ represents this door in spirit and in truth. He said that:

[8] *I know thy works: behold, I have set before thee an open door, and no man can shut it: for thou hast a little strength, and hast kept my word, and hast not denied my name.*
[20] *Behold, I stand at the door, and knock: if any man hear my voice, and open the door, I will come in to him, and will sup with him, and he with me*
Revelation 3: 8, 20

God himself sealed the ark at the only door that the ark contained, and the Holy Spirit sent by the Son of God now seals us into the body of Jesus Christ. This interpretation is made sure by the immediate comments of Peter. Peter said that *baptism by water does not save us by the putting away of the filth of the flesh but by the resurrection of Jesus Christ* (I Peter 3: 21. No amount of water can save anyone.... Baptism by water is a *physical* act only. True baptism is *Spiritual* when the Holy Spirit baptizes us into the body of Christ (After accepting Jesus Christ as Lord and Savior, every true believer receives the gift of the Holy Spirit, and is Baptized by the Holy Spirit into the Body of Christ (I Corinthians 12: 12-13). Baptized into the body of Christ means we are risen with Him to newness of life (Romans 6:4). We become a part of the perfect and sinless body of Christ, and are therefore acceptable to God. The physical act of water baptism can never bring about Spiritual baptism.

> Peter links our Spiritual baptism by the Holy Spirit to the story of Noah, using the physical waters of the flood as a type of the physical waters of baptism. Noah was *saved through water*. Noah was in the ark, going through the water (of the flood), as we are in Christ, going through the water (of baptism). The water did not save Noah, the ark did. The difference is that Noah's salvation through the ark was temporary, while our salvation through Christ is eternal.   *Got questions website*

The same analogy of water baptism was later used to type the miracle which took place as the nation of Israel passed through the Red Sea and was rescued by God. It was not the washing of water that saved Israel, but the act of every Israelite walking on dry land as they crossed the Red Sea. By faith they believed that the waters would not return until they had all passed through, and that it would be stayed by the hand of God.

The ordinance of baptism as a path to salvation is not found in the Old Testament, but there are biblical events that represented a type of baptism, and those events eventually found fulfillment in New Testament practice. Water has been an important religious symbol throughout biblical history: The Israelites under Joshua entered the Promised Land through the waters of the Jordan River; Elisha began his ministry after the rapture of Elijah by passing through the waters of the Jordan; John the Baptist called for repentance shown through baptism, and every Christian since Jesus' ascension has used baptism to show their repentance from sin and faith in Christ. The questions which arise are: (1) Is water baptism really an ordinance commanded by God, (2) Is Baptism part of God's plan for salvation? And, (3) Was water baptism taught by the apostle Paul when he revealed the *mystery* of the New Covenant?

Jewish Practice of Baptism Under the Law

After God rescued His people from the pursuing Egyptians and the Egyptian Pharoah, the new nation of Israel continued on to Mt. Sinai where God gave them the Law. Central to the law was the 10 commandments which were a set of *biblical principles relating to ethics and worship* that play a key role in both Judaism and Christianity. The ten commandments which God gave to Israel on tablets of stone were the first 10 of the 613 commandments given by God to the Jewish people. They form the foundation of Jewish ethics, as well as Jewish civil and religious law. God made a *conditional covenant* with Israel.

God told his chosen people, the Jews, that if they would obey His statutes and laws that He would bless them and make them the envy of the entire world. He gave them His laws (10 commandments) and His ordinances (603 commands) as the conditions that must be followed to prosper and to flourish as his chosen people (Amos 3:2, Isaiah 42:6. Deuteronomy 28:1).

[3] *If ye walk in my statutes, and keep my commandments, and do them;*
[4] *Then I will give you rain in due season, and the land shall yield her increase, and the trees of the field shall yield their fruit.*
[5] *And your threshing shall reach unto the vintage, and the vintage shall reach unto the sowing time: and ye shall eat your bread to the full, and dwell in your*

land safely.

[6] And I will give peace in the land, and ye shall lie down, and none shall make you afraid: and I will rid evil beasts out of the land, neither shall the sword go through your land.   Leviticus 26 3-5

[14] But if ye will not hearken unto me, and will not do all these commandments;
[15] And if ye shall despise my statutes, or if your soul abhor my judgments, so that ye will not do all my commandments, but that ye break my covenant:
[16] I also will do this unto you; I will even appoint over you terror, consumption, and the burning ague, that shall consume the eyes, and cause sorrow of heart: and ye shall sow your seed in vain, for your enemies shall eat it
Leviticus 26:14-16

The blessings (and curses) found under the Old Covenant depended on Israel's obedience. If they followed His laws and ordinances...... they would be blessed. If they disobeyed and followed after the fleshly ways of Satan and man...... they would be cursed. In this sense, the covenant is *conditional*. The conditional promises which God gave to Israel should not be confused with the *unconditional promises* which God made to Abraham.

[1] Now the LORD had said unto Abram, Get thee out of thy country, and from thy kindred, and from thy father's house, unto a land that I will shew thee:
[2] And I will make of thee a great nation, and I will bless thee, and make thy name great; and thou shalt be a blessing:
[3] And I will bless them that bless thee, and curse him that curse thee: and in thee shall all families of the earth be blessed   Genesis 12:1-

This is why that even though God turned his face away from the Jews during the Assyrian and Babylonian exile.... allowed the holocaust to occur under Hitler... and destroyed temple worship in 70 AD.... The Jews continue to exist for almost 4000 years.

Part of God's Commandments to Israel were concerned with water baptism.

The Mikvah

When Moses was given the 10 commandments concerning how the Children of Israel should live, they were also given the tabernacle. The movable tabernacle was later replaced by the permanent structure called Solomon's Temple and Herod's Temple as a permanent place to worship. Solomon's Temple was destroyed in 586 BC by the Babylonian Empire and Herod's Temple was destroyed by Titus and his Roman soldiers in 70 AD. From the beginning, God insisted that the Levitical Priesthood had to be ritually clean before offering sacrifices to God and the offeror had to be ritually clean to participate in the temporary covering of sin at the Altar of sacrifice. The ceremonial cleansing which was required were known as the *Mikvah*.

The ritualistic Laws of the Mikvah ceremony can be found in many Jewish rabbinical essays, but the fundamental purpose of the Mikvah at the Altar of Sacrifice is given by God in Leviticus 14. The High priest could not sacrifice any Sin or Trespass offerings to God until he was ritually clean. Likewise, the offer could not bring his/her offerings for sin to the Alter of Sacrifice until they were also ritually clean. This was accomplished by removing their clothes and totally immersing themselves in water (Mikvah). These acts of worship were a type of those currently exercised by Christians and Christian denominations. Under the law, these ordinances were only temporary and had to be repeated day after day. Under the New Covenant, the sacrifice of Jesus Christ for our sins at the Cross of Calvary as the perfect and final sacrifice for sins was final and complete. So, what is the New Covenant requirement for baptism?

Immediately preceding the 3.5-year ministry of reconciliation by Jesus Christ, John was baptizing in the River Jordan. We must be very careful to ask two important questions as we read the account of John the Baptizer in Matthew 3: (1) What was the purpose of John's baptism? (2) Who was being baptized?

John the Baptist

A cousin of Jesus Christ (John) was baptizing Jews to *repentance* (Mark 1:4) in the River Jordan. The written record of his ministry is in John 1 and Matthew 3. One day as he was baptizing, he looked down the road and saw Jesus coming. In joy he declared:

[29] *Behold the Lamb of God, which taketh away the sin of the world.*
[30] *This is he of whom I said: After me cometh a man which is preferred before me: for He was before me.*
[31] *And I knew him not: but that He should be made manifest to Israel, therefore am I come baptizing with water.*   John 1: 29-31

[5] *Then went out to him Jerusalem, and all Judaea, and all the region round about Jordan,*
[6] *And were baptized of him in Jordan, confessing their sins.*

[7] But when he saw many of the Pharisees and Sadducees come to his baptism, he said unto them, O generation of vipers, who hath warned you to flee from the wrath to come?
[8] Bring forth therefore fruits meet for repentance:
[9] And think not to say within yourselves, We have Abraham to our father: for I say unto you, that God is able of these stones to raise up children unto Abraham.
[10] And now also the axe is laid unto the root of the trees: therefore every tree which bringeth not forth good fruit is hewn down, and cast into the fire.
*[11] **I indeed baptize you with water unto repentance**: but he that cometh after me is mightier than I, whose shoes I am not worthy to bear: he shall baptize you with the Holy Ghost, and with fire*:   Matthew 3: 5-11

We will never understand the Baptism of John without recognizing that John was baptizing only Jews, and that it was a baptism of *repentance* to prepare the way for a redeemer who would be sent by God atone the sins of Israel. John 1:31 confirms that the baptism of John had nothing to do with salvation…... it was a baptism to prepare them for redemption and salvation by Jesus Christ; who would baptize them (the Jews) with *both* the *Holy Spirit* and with *fire* (Matthew 5:11).

> *Authors Comment:* Note that if water baptism is actually a sacred sacrament, in Matthew 5:11 there are 3 different baptisms mentioned and only one is water……and it is for repentance.

There is not even a hint that John or Jesus Christ was to baptize anyone into salvation. Salvation would come by remission of sins through the sacrificial death of Jesus Christ on the Cross of Calvary. Only Jesus Christ could redeem Israel from the curse of the law and everyone who would ever live from the curse of sin. He now reigns in heaven as our great High Priest. He ended the Levitical sacrificial system and replaced salvation under the law by works with salvation by faith and grace. With no further need of either the temple or the work of the Levitical priesthood, God removed both in 70 AD.

John the Baptist was offering water baptism to *only Jews* in the River Jordan. His baptism was a baptism of repentance to prepare the way for Jesus Christ. It had nothing to do with the Mikvah or the Levitical sacrificial system. So, why was Christ baptized by John? He was sinless and required no repentance. What was John's reaction when he saw Jesus coming?

[13] Then cometh Jesus from Galilee to Jordan unto John, to be baptized of him.
[14] But John forbad him, saying, I have need to be baptized of thee, and now you

come to me?
*[15] And Jesus answering said unto him; Suffer it to be so now: for thus it becometh us to **fulfil all righteousness**. Then he suffered him.*   Matthew 3: 13-15

Christ answered the first question Himself. He commanded John to baptize Him not for repentance but to *fulfil all righteousness.* By being baptized, Jesus was preparing Himself for 3.5 years of Priestly service to the Jews by going through a *Mikvah*. It had nothing to do with either salvation or redemption: it was part of the Old Covenant Law. Jesus Christ had to do this because He lived a sinless life and fulfilled every *jot and title* of the law (Matthew 5:18).   The Bible does not record *anyone* being baptized by Jesus. New Testament Baptism is a sign that the person who has been baptized has committed to Jesus Christ. It is also a sign that as you are covered with water in like manner Jesus was buried in the grave, and as you rise from the water you also rise with Jesus Christ to everlasting life. This symbolism suggests that baptism by immersion might be the correct choice.

When John was baptizing in the River Jordan, it was for repentance in order to prepare the way for the Jewish Messiah (Jesus Christ) who's which was imminent and at the door. The baptism of Christ was a confirmation to all Jews that there was someone who was coming to forgive their sins….and that someone was Himself (John 1:33). Again, be very clear that the entire account of Jesus ministry in Matthew, Mark Luke and John was a record of Jesus Ministry only to the Jews! if you are not a Jew by birth, you are a Gentile. Notice what Jesus Christ told his disciples to do in Matthew 5.

[5] These twelve Jesus sent forth, and commanded them, saying: Go ye not into the way of the Gentiles, and into any city of the Samaritans enter ye not:
[6] But go rather to the lost sheep of the house of Israel   Matthew 12: 5-6

You may say that you have never heard that preached, but there it is in Jesus own words. Yes, the New Covenant was offered to Jews and Gentiles alike, but it was offered to the Jews first. The entire earthly ministry of Christ was to the Jews. It was not until after his sacrificial death, the day of Pentecost and the stoning of Steven did Christ choose the Apostle Paul to reveal the *mystery of the church* and the new covenant to *both* Jews and Gentiles. This is probably a startling fact to most new covenant believers. The Old Covenant did not end until the death of Christ on the cross of calvary. Until that time the law was still in effect. Under the Old Covenant, there were only two classes of people: *Jews and Gentiles*. Under the New Covenant, there are still only two classes of people: *believers and unbelievers*. Jesus Christ was born a Jew…lived as a Jew …and died as a Jew. His entire earthly ministry of 3.5 years was directed exclusively to the Jews (Matthew 10:5). The Books of Matthew, Mark, Luke and John were all written to chronicle and record His earthly ministry to the Jews (Acts 28:28). Now, if Christ was speaking to the Jews only, was He speaking to you? Of course not, no more than to ask if God was speaking to the church today when He spoke to Adam and Eve. This entire line of reasoning means that the Books of Matthew, Mark Luke and John actually end the Age of the Law and the Old Covenant…not begin the New Covenant. This of course does not mean that the New Covenant Church believer today cannot learn from Matthew, Mark, Luke and John…who incidentally all tell the same story. Jesus himself said:

Think not that I am come to destroy the law, or the prophets: I am not come to destroy, but to fulfil (the law)   Matthew 5:10

A good example of this truth is the entire body of Matthew 24 and Matthew 25. This is called the *Olivet Discourse*. It was spoken to His Jewish disciples (Luke was probably a Hellenized Jew and he was likely converted to Judaism at an early Age). The body of Matthew 24 and 25 was to answer the following 3 questions as Jesus left the Temple in Jerusalem just 2 days before his last Passover Feast.

[1] And Jesus went out, and departed from the temple: and his disciples came to him for to shew him the buildings of the temple.
[2] And Jesus said unto them, See ye not all these things? verily I say unto you, There shall not be left here one stone upon another, that shall not be thrown down.
[3] And as he sat upon the mount of Olives, the disciples came unto him privately, saying, **Tell us, when shall these things be? and what shall be the sign of thy coming, and of the end of the world?**   Matthew 24:1-3

He chose to answer the last question but not the first two. His answer covered events which would not happen to the Jews until over 2000 years would pass. His answer revealed nothing about the Church Age since the New Covenant would not begin until Christ died on the Cross of Calvary. The church Age was a ***mystery*** to Jews at that time (including His disciples), and was a mystery until the Apostle Paul was chosen by God to reveal the good news of the gospel. This is a great truth and not well understood by Christians or Jews. When Christ died upon the Cross of Calvary, God temporarily *blinded Israel in part* and set aside the Jews until the fulness of the Gentiles should be completed (Romans 11:25). Of course, God did not completely abandon the Jews…he offered salvation by faith and grace to Jews and Gentiles alike. The Olivet Discourse was given to the Jews to reveal the final fate of the Jewish nation. The Church Age created a *gap* in Gods intimate relationship with the Jews. This gap would continue until the Great Tribulation begins and continue through the 1000-year Millennial Kingdom during which the Jews will inherit the land of Canaan as promised to Abraham and his seed. In both the ancient prophetic Book of Daniel, the Books of Matthew-Mark-Luke and John; and in the Olivet Discourse; the Church Age was completely unknown and hidden in God's heart (Romans 16:25). Jesus Christ in Matthew 24 and Matthew 25 completely skipped the church Age during which He would be dealing almost exclusively with the Gentiles. It is impossible to understand the last 3.5 years of this Age (Great Tribulation) and the 7th dispensation of time (the Millennial Kingdom) …… without understanding and studying his response. Although He was speaking only to Jews, we can learn much from what He prophesied at that time (See Phillips, *The Book of Revelation: Mysteries Revealed*).

Matthew 28:19

Matthew 28:19 is usually quoted by anyone who teaches or preaches that baptism is required of all New Covenant believers.

*Go ye therefore, and teach all nations, **baptizing** them in the name of the Father, and of the Son, and of the Holy Ghost*   Matthew 28:19

Now this is very clear.... Christ commanded His disciples to go forth and baptize all who would believe upon His name…. or did He? Well, yes and no.

Recall that there are 3 questions which must always be asked concerning the meaning of any scripture or set of scriptures in the Word of God: (1) Who is speaking? (2) What is being said? And (3) Who is being spoken to?

(1) *Who is speaking?*........Jesus Christ
(2) *What is being said?*... That the disciples were to go to all nations and baptize those who would believe.
(3) *Who is being spoken to?* ……Jews (the disciples)

Now, carefully note the context of what Christ said: He had previously directed all of his 12 disciples to go unto only the Jews…Not to the Gentiles.

*These twelve Jesus sent forth, and commanded them, saying: Go **not** into the way of the **Gentiles**, and into any city of the Samaritans enter ye not*   Matthew 10:5

Is Jesus through His chosen 12 disciples speaking to Gentiles? ..... *NO*. The fact is that the Church (body of Christ) and the details of the New Covenant were completely unknown when Matthew 28:19 took place. Notice that This command was given to His disciples *before* He went to the cross and offered salvation to *both* Jews and Gentiles. Matthew 28:19 cannot possibly apply to New Covenant believers. He was commanding His disciples to baptize Jews by John's baptism of *repentance*, just as John the Baptizer was baptizing Jews to repentance. Is Christ at this time speaking to the church at all…....NO. Christ is speaking only to the Jews. there is no other possible interpretation of what Christ commanded his disciples to do……and who He was speaking to. This is *exactly* what the apostle Paul revealed concerning how to study and rightly interpret all scripture.

*Study to shew thyself approved unto God, a workman that needs not to be ashamed, rightly **dividing** the word of truth*   II Timothy 2:15

Rightly dividing the Word of God demands that the previous three questions be asked of every verse in the bible, and it requires an understanding that the Holy Words of God can only be understood by recognizing that the Holy Bible is a dispensational document. A key to understanding the New Covenant is to realize that the Gospels of Matthew-Mark-Luke and John were all written records of events that took place under the Old Covenant, not the New Covenant. Jesus and Matthew-mark-Luke and John were speaking to Jews, not gentiles and the Church Age had not even begun.

Three Types of Old Testament Baptism

We have already discussed Baptism in the Old Testament as a way to cleanse the Levitical priesthood and the people as they offered up the blood of sacrificial bulls and goats to cover (atone) their sins at the Altar of Sacrifice. Baptism was not optional; it was demanded by the law. Paul revealed in his letter to the Hebrews that: *it is not possible that the **blood** of bulls and of goats should take away sins* (Hebrews 10:4). The entire sacrificial system, including Old Testament baptism, was a type of the atoning and redemptive work of Jesus Christ. When the glory of Jesus Christ was come, shadows and types of things to come passed away. In Matthew 3, the Apostle John revealed that the Baptism of Repentance would soon be replaced by two other types of baptism.

*I indeed baptize you with water unto repentance: but he that cometh after me is mightier than I, whose shoes I am not worthy to bear: he shall baptize you with the **Holy Ghost**, and with **fire***   Matthew 3:11

Once again, recognize that this revelation and prophecy by John was to the Jews and not to the Gentiles. The Apostle John told the Jews that his baptism of repentance would be replaced by a baptism by the *Holy Ghost* and by *fire*. When did this happen? It happened on the Day of Pentecost 50 days after Christ rose from the dead. Jews from every nation were gathered at the temple in Jerusalem to attend the Feast of Pentecost. As Peter urged the Jews to repent and accept Jesus Christ as their long-awaited redeemer, the **Holy Ghost** fell upon those Jews who were standing there.

[1] *And when the day of Pentecost was fully come, they were all with one accord in one place.*
[2] *And suddenly there came a sound from heaven as of a rushing mighty wind, and it filled all the house where they were sitting.*
[3] *And there appeared unto them* **cloven tongues like as of fire**, *and it sat upon each of them.*
[4] *And they were* **all filled with the Holy Ghost**, *and* **began to speak with other tongues**, *as the Spirit gave them utterance* Acts 2:1-4

Jews from all over the world were gathered in Jerusalem speaking many languages and many dialects. These Jews who were from all over the known world and they were not babbling unintelligible words, but speaking to other Jews in their own native languages (Acts 2:6). As each became filled with the Holy Spirit they supernaturally began to speak in other languages. The Jewish Pharisees and Sadducees were astounded and said: *Look, they are all drunk with wine* (Acts 2:13). Peter responded as follows:

[15] *For these are not drunken, as ye suppose, seeing it is but the third hour of the day.*
[16] *But this is that which was spoken by the prophet* **Joel**;
[17] *And it shall come to pass in the last days, saith God: I will pour out of my Spirit upon all flesh: and your sons and your daughters shall prophesy, and your young men shall see visions, and your old men shall dream dreams:*
[18] *And on my servants and on my handmaidens I will pour out in those days of my Spirit; and they shall prophesy:* Acts 2: 15-18

If we examine the context of Acts 2: 1-18 and what Joel prophesied in Joel 2: 28-29, it is clear that his prophecy was not fulfilled on that day. Joel without controversy was speaking of things which would occur not only on the Day of Pentecost but at the second coming of Christ. So how could Peter relate what happened on the Day of Pentecost to things that would take place at the second coming of Christ? The Book of Joel says a number of things must happen before his prophecies can be fulfilled. None of them has yet happened. Therefore, if one argues for a literal and total fulfillment of the prophecy of Joel it is something which remains in the future. Regardless of why and how Peter explained what happened on the Day of Pentecost in 30 AD it was something that happened to Jews and not Gentiles that were all gathered in Jerusalem at that time.

Having rightly discerned and divided the context of Christ's words in Matthew, Mark, Luke and John……What is the role of Baptism under the New Covenant?

Baptism in the New Testament During the Age of Grace

To understand the role of baptism in the New Testament and the church today, one must recognize that after the Day of Pentecost in 30 AD, the Apostle Paul was chosen by the risen Christ on the Road to Damascus to reveal the new plan of salvation to the entire world. Just as Moses spoke for God to the Jews in the Old Testament, Paul spoke for God to both Jews and Gentiles in the New Testament (his primary calling was to the Gentiles…... Romans 11:13). He revealed that salvation would now be offered to Jews and Gentiles alike by faith and grace. Salvation would come through the sacrificial death of Jesus Christ who was born to the virgin Mary to escape Adam's curse. He was born sinless…...lived a sinless life…and died sinless: all as a Jew. He was both the offerer of a perfect sacrifice and the offered sacrifice. Every drop of his precious blood was shed for you and I, and by His death God would accept that sacrifice for the sins of the whole world…...Past, present and future. But that was not all, by his death and through His blood the Old Covenant passed away. No one could live a sinless life under the Law……. All had sinned and the *wages of sin is death*……. Spiritual death, and eternal separation from God and Jesus Christ. It was necessary that Christ would come and be crucified for the sins of the world. Man was not capable of living under the law. That does not mean that the laws of God were not good and Holy, but that when those laws are broken under the New Covenant, they would not condemn man to death. God's plan to save mankind was spectacular and unique

[16] *For God so loved the* **world**, *that he gave his only begotten Son, that whosoever believeth in him should not perish, but have everlasting life.*
[17] *For God sent not his Son into the* **world** *to condemn the* **world**; *but that the* **world** *through him might be saved.*   John 3:16-17

How wonderful it is to know that our sins will not condemn us to a spiritual death, but they have been bought and paid for by Jesus Christ. Every born-again Christian is a *new creature* in Jesus Christ. Every Old Covenant man/woman of faith and every New Covenant believer is no longer cursed and condemned by the first man Adam, but is saved by faith and love by the second man…. Jesus Christ.

[45] And so it is written: The first man Adam was made a living soul; the last Adam was made a quickening Spirit.
[46] Howbeit that was not first which is Spiritual, but that which is natural; and afterward that which is Spiritual.
[47] The first man is of the earth, earthy: the second man is the Lord from heaven
   I Corinthians 15: 45-47

There is therefore now no condemnation to them which are in Christ Jesus, who walk not after the flesh, but after the Spirit   Romans 8:1

It is interesting and instructive to understand that water Baptism does not play a role in New Covenant salvation. It is not mandatory and was not commanded by Christ who spoke to the church and the Body of Christ through the Apostle Paul. The word *baptism* is found 23 times in the New Testament: Ten times in Matthew-Mark-Luke and John, which we have shown was spoken to the Jews, and 7 times in the Book of Acts, which in every case refers to the John's Baptism of repentance to the Jews. The apostle Paul used the word baptism in only 5 of his 13 epistles to the Church and in every instance, he was referring back to John's baptism of repentance to the Jews. Hence, in every usage the word *baptism* was used to reference John's baptism for repentance to the Jews. All 12 apostles were commanded by Christ to go unto the Jews and proclaim the good news. Baptism by each apostle followed the baptism of Christ that He received of John the Baptizer in the River Jordan.

*[1] When therefore the Lord knew how the Pharisees had heard that Jesus made and **baptized** more disciples than John,*
*[2] (Though Jesus himself **baptized** not, but his disciples*   John 4: 1-2

Jesus Christ did not baptize with water, but John did and his disciples did. If baptism was important to Jesus Christ, the author and the finisher of our salvation……He certainly did not emphasize it, and neither did Paul (I Corinthians 1: 13-17). On the other hand, Paul did teach that every New Covenant believer would experience a Holy Ghost baptism.

For John truly baptized with water; but ye shall be baptized with the Holy Ghost not many days hence   Acts 1:5

We will shortly prove from the scriptures that New Covenant baptism is by the Holy Spirit into the body of Christ. It is a *spiritual* act of faith and not a *physical* act.

It is worth carefully noting what Peter said in I Peter 3.

> *... whereunto even baptism doth also now save us (not the putting away of the filth of the flesh, but the answer of a good conscience toward God,) by the resurrection of Jesus Christ*   I Peter 3:21

Those who teach and believe that baptism is necessary for salvation use I Peter 3:21 as a proof text that baptism does save us. Like every other verse in the Holy Bible, one verse cannot be in conflict with another, and the Holy Bible is clear that salvation comes by faith and grace in Jesus Christ (Ephesians 2: 8-9). Peter was chosen by God to offer salvation to the Jews, and the epistle of I Peter was written to the Jews, not the Gentiles. Peter is not implying in any way that Baptism will save anyone, but that the Jews must accept and experience the baptism of repentance by John before they can be saved by the atoning death of Jesus Christ.

The proof that this is the true meaning of I Peter 3:2 is in examining closely what Peter wrote and what he meant.

- 1.0 If baptism can save anyone, it would be in direct conflict with many other New Covenant teachings.
- 2.0 A normal and straightforward meaning of I Peter 1:1 suggests that Peter is writing to a Jewish audience
- 3.0 His criticism of the Jews in I Peter 1:14 and I Peter 1:18 is language appropriate for Hellenistic Jews, and parallels what Paul wrote in Romans 10: 2-3.
- 4.0 The words of Peter in I Peter 2:12 and I Peter 4: 3-4 seem to imply that he was not writing for a Gentile audience.

Every Jew who is saved by faith and grace before Pentecost was saved by: (1) First receiving the baptism of repentance by the water baptism of John…...Acts 2:38 (2) After repenting (turning around and going in another direction), each Jew is saved in exactly the same way that every gentile is saved….by faith in what is called their redeemer, who was Jesus Christ…..Acts 2:44. Every Jew who accepted Jesus Christ on the Day of Pentecost by the Faith of Abraham, was baptized to repentance and received the Holy Spirit was saved at that time. This is quite different from the message that the Apostle John gave to the Body of Christ. Every person who is saved by faith immediately *receives* the Spirit of promise and is *sealed* with that same Spirit. It is also by that same Spirit that a true believer is *baptized* into the body of Christ (Acts 1:3, Acts 2:38, Acts 11:16, Romans 6:3, I Corinthians 12:13).

Consider Peter in Acts 10: 43-47. Peter is speaking to a gentile named Cornelius (Acts 10:25). He had sought out Peter in his house after becoming a follower of Jesus. As Peter talked with Cornelius, suddenly the Holy Ghost fell upon him and others who were there (Acts 10:44). Peter then declared that since they had all been filled with the Holy Spirit that it was proper that they should all be baptized. Baptism was an act of confirmation of repentance, and it was followed by remission of sins by faith (Acts 10:43). The context and the passage are very clear; Cornelius and his household received both forgiveness of sins and the Holy Spirit before they were ever baptized. In fact, the reason Peter suggested that they be baptized was that they showed evidence of receiving the Holy Spirit *just as Peter and other Jewish believers had* (Acts 10:47).

Previously, Peter had encountered a group of *Jews* who had gathered in Jerusalem for the Feast of Pentecost (Acts 2:5). As they heard Peter preaching the Gospel, they were moved to ask Peter how they could be saved (Acts 2:37). Peter replied that they must: (1) Repent (2) Receive John's baptism in water of repentance and then (3) They would receive the Holy Spirit. This is a different sequence than when Peter spoke to Cornelius in Acts 10. Why was this? In Acts 2 those who were saved were all *Jews* and those in Acts 10 were all *Gentiles*. Note what Peter told the Jews in Acts 2.

Then Peter said unto them, Repent, and be baptized every one of you in the name of Jesus Christ for the remission of sins, and ye shall receive the gift of the Holy Ghost   Acts 2:38

All references to water baptism before the Day of Pentecost were to Jews who were baptized unto *repentance.* After the Feast of Pentecost, Jews and Gentiles were baptized by the *Holy Spirit.* Some Jews followed after Christ, believed that He was the Son of God and that He was their promised redeemer……but did not receive the Holy Spirit until much later (Acts 19: 2-6). These acts of Baptism which concerned the Jews should not be confused with the baptism which Paul revealed to the Gentiles and to the body of Christ.

The Apostle Paul and His Message to the Church (Body of Christ)

The Apostle Paul was chosen by God to reveal the New Covenant…. His message was that salvation had come to *both* Jews and Gentiles…not by the works of the law but by grace and faith. He wrote 13 epistles to reveal the New Covenant and how we (Christians) should live under grace. The term *Christians* was first used in the Church at Antioch by Paul (Acts 11:26). He was chosen by God to reveal the New Covenant to the Gentiles, and his message to New Covenant believers was a *mystery* which was not known before his ministry. A mystery is something which was not previously known or understood until it is revealed. The entire Church Age and the New Covenant was completely unknown in Ages past.

[26] *Even the **mystery** which hath been hid from Ages and from generations, but now is made manifest to his saints:*
[27] *To whom God would make known what is the riches of the glory of this **mystery** among the Gentiles; which is Christ in you, the hope of glory*
Colossians 1:26-27

*This is a great **mystery**: but I speak concerning Christ and the church*
Ephesians 5:32

[3] *How that by revelation he made known unto me the **mystery**; (as I wrote afore in few words,*
[4] *Whereby, when ye read, ye may understand my knowledge in the **mystery** of Christ*   Ephesians 3: 3-4

What Did Paul say about Baptism?

In I Corinthians 1:17 Paul made the following statement.

[17] *For **Christ sent me not to baptize**, but to preach the gospel: not with wisdom of words, lest the cross of Christ should be made of none effect.*
[18] *For the preaching of the cross is to them that perish foolishness; but unto us which are saved it is the power of God*   I Corinthians 1:17

If Paul wrote his 13 epistles to the church (body of Christ) on how to be saved and lead a new life in Christ…It is strange that He did not baptize everyone that received Christ as their Lord and Savior but only a selected few. Paul said: *I thank God I baptized none of you, save a few, and that Christ sent me not to baptize, but to preach the gospel* (I Corinthians 1:17). If Paul thought that Baptism was required of every new believer, you can bet that he would have baptized everyone. Realize that the Baptism of John was to *repentance*, to prepare the Jews for Jesus Christ. If Paul *would have* required baptism for salvation, then it would contradict many scriptures that salvation under the New

Covenant was based upon *faith*. In Mark 16:16 and in Acts 2: 36-41 it appears that Baptism is necessary to be saved, however, recall that this command was to the Jews.... The baptism was one of repentance...and this was before the cross and the New Covenant. This is best summed up by Paul in his epistle to the Romans.

[3] For what saith the scripture? Abraham believed God, and it was counted unto him for righteousness.
[4] Now to him that worketh is the reward not reckoned of grace, but of debt.
[5] But to him that worketh not, but believeth on him that justifies the ungodly, his faith is counted for righteousness   Romans 4: 3-5

If these passages had intended to make water baptism a requirement for salvation, then the Bible would be contradicting itself, and we know that God never contradicts Himself (1Samuel 15:29). The Jews were instructed by John the Baptizer to be baptized by water before the New Covenant began at the cross, and Paul taught that under the New Covenant the *Holy Spirit* will baptize every Christian (Jew or Gentile) into the body of Christ. Paul talks about this baptism in Romans 6: 3-4, I Corinthians 12:13, Galatians 3:27, Ephesians 4:5, and Colossians 2:12. These are all references to work done by the Holy Spirit in the heart of every believer. Every born-again Christian receives the Holy Spirit which then leads the true-believer into what which we call the *baptism of the Holy Spirit,* or what is called baptism by the Holy Ghost. Baptism by the Holy Spirit results in us being changed into a new creature in Christ. We become a part of Christ and are heirs to all His promises since Christ cannot deny Himself. Water baptism is merely a physical sign of something greater. Paul teaches in Romans 6 and I Corinthians 15 that water baptism is a picture of how we died with Christ through the baptism of the Holy Spirit, and how we will rise from the grave one day just as He did. When we experience water baptism by going under the surface of the water, we affirm our Spiritual death as we join into the physical death of Jesus Christ upon the Cross of Calvary (*i.e.*, going down into the grave with Christ). When we come up out of the water, we affirm our future resurrection in Christ. Therefore, the act of water baptism is an outward sign of the inward change accomplished by the baptism of the Holy Spirit.

The Baptism of Paul...What was It?

Paul was spreading the gospel throughout all the known world, and we have seen how he was not administering water baptism except on special occasions (I Corinthians 1: 14-17). Water baptism was just not that important to Paul, but why? One reason why he did not baptize new believer was that there were those in the Church at Corinth which were elevating themselves into positions of authority because they were baptizing all new believers. Paul was always very sensitive and worried about how people viewed his ministry. On every occasion, he minimized himself and maximized Jesus Christ. His focus was always on Christ, and he taught that only Christ was the *way,* the *truth* and the *life……no man cometh unto the Father except by Him*. This might have been the motivation for Paul to avoid baptizing the new believers that he won to Christ, but this was not the main reason. Paul knew that water baptism was not necessary for salvation, and the baptism of John was only a sign of repentance to prepare them for the appearance and message of Jesus Christ. Paul was a devout Jew (Philippians 3:5) who understood Judaism and the Law, but he knew that the New Covenant based upon faith and not works was superior in every way to the Old Covenant.

For Christ sent me not to baptize, but to preach the gospel: not with wisdom of words, lest the cross of Christ should be made of none effect   I Corinthians 1:17

When Paul says *Christ sent me not to baptize* (I Corinthians 1:17), he was confessing that he was not following Matthew (Matthew 28) or Mark (Mark 16) in his ministry, nor was he baptizing under the same command given to Peter. The Lord commanded his twelve apostles to teach the law and baptize all nations (Matthew 28:19-20). Peter's message was *repent and be baptized* by the baptism of John. Paul taught that every New Covenant Christian was not Baptized to repentance but was baptized by the Holy Spirit into the body of Christ (I Corinthians 12: 12-27).

Paul baptized Crispus (the chief ruler of the synagogue) in the name of the Lord Jesus (I Corinthians 1:14), but he was called not to baptize others so that the Corinthians would know that the power of God unto salvation is in the gospel of Christ, and not in the baptisms of Peter, Apollos, or Paul (I Corinthians1: 13-17). The Lord revealed to him the mystery of one baptism by one Spirit, and that all New covenant believers are identified as one body of Christ (Ephesians 4:4-6, I Corinthians 12:13). The Holy Spirit not only baptizes every Christian into the Body of Christ, but His Spirit seals you for that day when you will be raised from the dead to dwell with Him forever. The Lord himself separated Paul to preach this mystery of Christ.

Baptism by the Holy Spirit

[9] *But ye are not in the flesh, but in the Spirit, if so be that the Spirit of God dwell*

in you. Now if any man has not the Spirit of Christ, he is none of his.
[10] And if Christ be in you, the body is dead because of sin; but the Spirit is life because of righteousness.
[11] But if the Spirit of him that raised up Jesus from the dead dwell in you, he that raised up Christ from the dead shall also **quicken your mortal bodies** *by his Spirit that dwelleth in you*   Romans 8: 9-11

[13] In whom ye also trusted, after that ye heard the word of truth, the gospel of your salvation: in whom also after that ye believed, **ye were sealed** *with that Holy Spirit of promise,*
[14] Which is the **earnest of our inheritance until the redemption** *of the purchased possession, unto the praise of his* glory   Ephesians 1: 13-14

Know ye not, that so many of us as were baptized into Jesus Christ were baptized into his death?   Romans 6:3

For by one Spirit are we all baptized into one body, whether we be Jews or Gentiles, whether we be bond or free; and have been all made to drink into one Spirit   I Corinthians 12:13

First Corinthians 12:13 is a central passage in the Bible regarding baptism. This scripture has nothing whatsoever to do with water baptism, nor does it imply that all Christians must be baptized for salvation. It refers to when a born-again Christian commits His/her life to Christ, that person receives the gift of the Holy spirit, and is then baptized by that same Holy spirit into the Body of Christ. Baptism of the Holy Spirit does two things: (1) It joins us to the body of Christ, and (2) It affirms that if He was raised from the dead, then we will be also. Being in His body means we are risen with Him to newness of life (Romans 6:4). Experiencing Spirit Baptism serves as the basis for keeping unity in the church (Ephesians 4: 3-5). Being associated with Christ in His death, burial, and resurrection through Spirit baptism establishes the basis for our separation from the power of indwelling sin, and strengthens our walk in newness of life (Romans 6:1-10; Colossians 2:12).

Summary and Biblical Truth

This study of God's Holy word is not intended to prove that water baptism in any form is not good and righteous, it is intended to emphatically show that water baptism is not required to gain eternal life in Jesus Christ. It is a physical act of rebirth in Jesus Christ. It is the confirmation that one has believed in faith that Jesus Christ died on the Cross of Calvary, and that by His sacrificial death He did away with the law and salvation by works. New Covenant baptism by water is an outward sign that an inner change has taken place. It is a confirmation that you are a new person in Jesus Christ, having been placed into Christ by the Holy Spirit. By that regeneration, we are heirs to all of the promises of Christ. He was crucified, dead and buried, and He and rose from the grave to eternal glory with His Father. When the Holy Spirit baptizes any New Believer into Christ, we are born-again.

The Sign of a Christian and the New Covenant

In order to identify the sign of a New Covenant believer, it is necessary to once again establish the Biblical and historical role of a sign, we have learned in Chapter 2 that God is a *Covenant Keeping* God who cannot fail to keep His promises to man. The world was once renovated by a great flood from which only 8 were saved. God made a covenant with Noah that He would never again destroy all flesh upon the earth by water and that a sign would be the rainbow.

But with thee will I establish my covenant; and thou shalt come into the ark, thou, and thy sons, and thy wife, and thy sons' wives with thee   Genesis 6:18

....and the LORD said in his heart, I will not again curse the ground any more for man's sake; for the imagination of man's heart is evil from his youth; neither will I again smite any more everything living, as I have done   Genesis 8:21

And I, behold, I establish my covenant with you, and with your seed after you

[11] And I will establish my covenant with you; neither shall all flesh be cut off any more by the waters of a flood; neither shall there any more be a flood to destroy the earth.
[12] And God said, This is the token of the covenant which I make between me and you and every living creature that is with you, for perpetual generations:
[13] I do set my bow in the cloud, and it shall be for a token of a covenant between me and the earth.
Genesis 9:9, 11-13

When God chose Abraham to be the father of many nations, He established a covenant with him which was *unilateral*. The covenant that God made with Abraham was *unconditional*, and it was both spiritual and physical.

[1] Now the LORD had said unto Abram: Get thee out of thy country, and from thy kindred, and from thy father's house, unto a land that I will shew thee:
[2] And I will make of thee a great nation, and I will bless thee, and make thy name great; and thou shalt be a blessing:
[3] And I will bless them that bless thee, and curse him that curses thee: and in thee shall all families of the earth be blessed.   Genesis 12:1-3

[3] And Abram fell on his face: and God talked with him, saying,
[4] As for me, behold, my covenant is with thee, and thou shalt be a father of many nations.
[5] Neither shall thy name any more be called Abram, but thy name shall be Abraham; for a father of many nations have I made thee.
[6] And I will make thee exceeding fruitful, and I will make nations of thee, and kings shall come out of thee.
[7] And I will establish my covenant between me and thee and thy seed after thee in their generations for an everlasting covenant, to be a God unto thee, and to thy seed after thee.
[8] And I will give unto thee, and to thy seed after thee, the land wherein thou art a stranger, all the land of Canaan, for an everlasting possession; and I will be their God   Genesis 17: 3-8

This was called the *Abramic Covenant*, and it was in three parts.

   1. God would make from Abraham a great nation. God would bless Abraham and his offspring, and He would make his name great.
Abraham would be *blessed to be a be a blessing*, and God would bless those who bless him and curse him who curses him. All the people on earth would be blessed through Abraham.
   2. God promised to give Abraham's descendants all the land from the river of Egypt to the Euphrates. Later, this land came to be referred to as the *Promised Land*.
   3. Abraham was to become the father of many nations, and his progeny would be Kings and priests.

The sign of this unconditional covenant was by blood. Every male off spring was to be *circumcision* (Genesis 17:10).

God never abandoned either Abraham or Israel, and after 215 years of Egyptian slavery He heard their pleas and liberated them from Egypt. God reinforced the covenant that He had made with Abraham with the *Mosaic Covenant*. The Mosaic

Covenant was a *conditional* covenant made between God and the Nation of Israel at Mount Sinai (Exodus 19-24). The Mosaic Covenant was directly related to Israel's obedience to the Mosaic Law. If Israel was obedient, then God would bless them; but if they disobeyed His statutes and laws, then God would punish them. The blessings and curses that are associated with this conditional covenant are found in detail in Deuteronomy 28. The Mosaic Law would reveal to people their sinfulness and their need for a Savior, and it is the Mosaic Law that Christ said: *Think not that I am come to destroy the law, or the prophets: I am not come to destroy, but to fulfil the law* (Matthew 5:17). This is an important point because some people get confused by thinking that keeping the Law saved people in the Old Testament, but the Bible is clear that salvation has always been by faith alone. The *Mosaic Covenant* did not really take away sins (Hebrews 10: 1-4); it simply foreshadowed the bearing of sin by Christ, the perfect high priest who was also the perfect sacrifice for the sins of the world (Hebrews 9: 11-28). Therefore, the Mosaic Covenant itself, with all its detailed laws, could not save people.

For the law of the Spirit of life in Christ Jesus hath made me free from the law of sin and death   Romans 8:2

 It is not that there was any problem with the Law itself, for the Law is perfect and was given by a holy God, but the Law had no power to give people new life, and the people were not able to obey the Law (Galatians 3:21).

 When God established His conditional covenant with Moses and the people, at Mt. Sinai, He renewed the covenant that he had made with Abraham. and gave the people the Ten Commandments, which was a set of rules by which they should live. The *sign* of the Mosaic Covenant was still male circumcision.

After God chose King David to rule upon the throne of Solomon's Temple in Jerusalem, he made an *unconditional* covenant between God and David by which God promised David and Israel that the Messiah (Jesus Christ) would come from the lineage of David and the tribe of Judah. God also assured King David that: *I will establish the throne of David forever* (II Samuel 7:13), and: *Your house and your kingdom will endure forever before Me* (II Samuel 7:16). A prophesied Messiah and Son of David would rule forever. This is a reference to the Messiah, Jesus Christ, called the *Son of David* (Matthew 21:9). There is no *sign* of the Davidic covenant specifically mentioned in the biblical record, but if there is any visible symbol of God's covenant with King David it would be the *Ark of the Covenant*. If this was a sign, it disappeared when Herod's Temple was burned to the ground in 70 AD. Jewish belief is that the Ark of the covenant will be found and restored to a newly rebuilt Jewish temple when God returns to fulfil the Davidic Covenant. In 30 AD Jesus Christ established a new and better Covenant which replaced the Old Covenant. So, what is the *sign* of the *New Covenant*?

Sign of the New Covenant

When God instituted the Lord's Last Supper, he broke the bread and said: *This is my body which is given for you: this do in remembrance of me* (Luke 22:19). After the bread was eaten, Jesus took the wine and said something else which was very significant: *This cup is the New Testament in my blood, which is shed for you* (Luke 22:20). The Greek word translated as *Testament* is *diathe'ke'*, and it actually means *covenant* (Strong's #1242). Now, let us dismiss and reject that the bread and the wine were reconstituted as the body and blood of Christ as is taught by the Roman Catholic Church. The *bread* was symbolic of the broken body of Christ, and the *wine* was symbolic of the precious blood that Jesus Christ shed for the sins of the whole world on the Cross of Calvary.

What Jesus was saying at this last supper was that He would establish and ratify a New Covenant by the shedding of his precious blood, He was saying that it was the blood of Christ which covers our sins…. Jews and Gentiles alike. This was instituted as an everlasting, unconditional promise that salvation would be by *faith and grace*, and not by the works of the law. God established a new and better covenant by the sinless, sacrificial death of His son, Jesus Christ, and every time we observe communion, we should remember what Christ did and thank God.

Since there is no commandment or law that even remotely suggests that water baptism is necessary for salvation under the New Covenant, should it even be observed? In my opinion…. YES.

When anyone, Jew or Gentile, is *born again* by the Holy Spirit into the body of Jesus Christ.

For by one Spirit are we all baptized into one body, whether we be Jews or Gentiles, whether we be bond or free   I Corinthians 12:13

There is a supernatural and permanent transformation that takes place when anyone is born-again (John 3:3). Baptism is not required for salvation, but it is an outward sign of our belief in Jesus and that we have been baptized into Jesus Christ and that we have been crucified with Him (Philippians 1:21) It represents our union with Jesus in his death, burial and resurrection, and it signifies our birth into God's family, forgiveness of sins and our new life in the Holy Spirit that comes through faith in Jesus Christ.

A Jewish Baptism Site on the River Jordan

CHAPTER 3

Tithing

Tithing in a New Covenant church is a controversial and divisive topic, which is almost universally poorly taught and misunderstood in denominational churches today. It is not uncommon to hear a church pastor teach that a 10% tithe is required of all New Covenant believers, and failure to do so will result in being cursed and shunned by God. Conversely, it is also taught that if a person does tithe that he/she would be favored by God and that blessings would fill the tither's house. *Where did all of this come from and what is the New Testament teaching on tithing?*

To understand the meaning and obligation to tithe, it is necessary to answer the following three questions: (1) *Where tithing originated in the Holy Scriptures*? and (2) *How much was required?* (3) *What are the New Covenant commands to tithe?*

The Origin of Tithing

The first time that tithing is mentioned in the Old Testament is in Genesis 14.

[16] *And he* (Abram) *brought back all the goods, and also brought again his brother Lot, and his goods, and the women also, and the people.*
[17] *And the King of Sodom went out to meet him after his return from the slaughter of Chedorlaomer, and of the Kings that were with him, at the valley of Shaveh, which is the King's dale.*
[18] *And Melchizedek King of Salem brought forth bread and wine: and he was the priest of the most high God.*
[19] *And he blessed him, and said, Blessed be Abram of the most high God, possessor of heaven and earth*:
[20] *And blessed be the most high God, which hath delivered thine enemies into thy hand.* **And he gave him tithes of all**   Genesis 14: 16-20

The context of Genesis 14: 16-20 involves Abraham and Lot. Abraham and Lot were both very wealthy in the land of Canaan, and both had large herds of sheep and cattle. The time came when the land would not support both of their sheep and cattle, so Lot moved his household, his sheep and his cows to the Land of Hebron. After a while, 5 Kings of Chaldea and Persia coveted the land of Canaan. They united and attacked the Kings which lived there. They defeated the Kings which reigned over the land, and also captured Lot and all of his possessions. Hearing of Lot's plight, Abram (Abraham) went to help him. He defeated the Amorites and the Amalekites, rescued Lot and his family and recovered Lot's sheep and cattle. As he returned with the riches and spoils of war, Abram encountered the mysterious King of Salem (Jerusalem) called *Melchizedek*. Melchizedek was both a King and a High Priest of God. Abram honored Melchizedek by giving him a *tithe* of everything he had seized from the enemy (Hebrews 7:4).

The account of Genesis 4 is often given as proof that a tithe of 10% is required of all New Testament Christians. This is a very interesting story. *First*, this was *before the Law was given to Israel*, and there is no hint that a tithe of everything that Abram had seized in war was given to Melchizedek for any other reason than to honor him as a *man of God*. *Second*, the tithe that Abraham gave to Melchizedek was a gross tithe of all that Abraham had seized in battle. *Third*, the tithe is usually always specified as 10%, but this is never stated in Genesis 4. The amount of the tithe that Abraham gave to Melchizedek was not revealed in scripture until Hebrews 7:4. It should be noted that the Hebrew word for tithe is *ma'asar*, which means a *tenth*. In other words, this tithe was strictly to honor Melchizedek. There is no precedence for this event in the Holy Scriptures. It took place in the *Dispensation of New Beginnings*.

Tithing Under the Law of Moses

About 400 years later, God called Moses out of the Land of Midian along with Aaron his brother (Numbers 26:50). After causing 10 plagues to fall upon the Pharoah and the Egyptians, Moses and all of Israel were told to leave. Three days later, God liberated the Children of Israel by drowning a pursuing Pharoah and his army in the Red Sea. They then journeyed to Mt. Sinai where God gave the Law to Moses and the Children of Israel. The Law is generally regarded as the 10 commandments, but it was much broader and far reaching than that. God gave Israel about 113 laws to govern their religious, social and dietary activities. God also gave Moses's building instructions for the *tabernacle* and appointed the Levitical Priesthood to conduct the affairs of the Tabernacle. The commandments for *tithing* were also given to the people. It is not well known among pastors or New Covenant Christians, but God ordained 3 separate tithes for Israel and the Jews. The 3 different types of tithes are as follows.

(1) The Levitical, or *Sacred Tithe* (Numbers 18: 21- 24).
(2) The *Tithe for the Feasts* (Deuteronomy 14: 22-27)

(3) The Tithe for the Poor (Deuteronomy 14: 28-29)

The *Sacred Tithe*

When God gave Moses the blueprint for the Tabernacle, He also set apart the Levites for temple service. The Levites who served in the temple were Jewish males who were all descended from the tribe of Levy. Levy was the 3rd son of Jacob and Leah. There were 3 types of Levites who served in the temple: (1) The High Priest (2) The Royal Priesthood and (3) Ordinary Levites. When God dedicated the Tabernacle, He anointed the High Priest to preside over the priests and ordinary people. The *High priest* also managed the treasury (storehouse) in the temple. Every year on the *Day of Atonement* he would ritually cleanse himself by water baptism, put on the robes of righteousness, offer an animal as sacrifice for his sins and then enter the Holy of Holies to plea for the sins of the people. The *general priesthood* would:

- Teach the gospel.
- Baptize.
- Administer the sacrament.
- Visit the members.
- Ordain others to the Aaronic Priesthood.

The *ordinary Levites* were tasked with singing Psalms during Temple services, perform construction and maintenance for the Temple, act as guards, and perform other services to support the priesthood. Levites also served as teachers and judges, ruling over *cities of refuge* in biblical times.

God made an *Unconditional Covenant* with Abraham, and later confirmed to Moses and King David that 12 tribes of Israel would someday inherit and live in *all* of the Land of Canaan. This will not take place until the 1000-year Millennial Kingdom (the 7th Dispensation) begins. The Levites had the Lord as their inheritance, and so they were promised no land. Since the Levites inherited no land, they would have no means to raise crops or own cattle and sheep. Hence, God commanded that every male Jew would dedicate 10% of their increase each year to the Levitical priesthood. This tithe was to be brought to the temple once a year, and the agricultural increase and any profit from the sale of agriculture or herds were to be placed in the *storehouse*, where they would be distributed by the High Priest. The storehouse became synonymous with the Temple but is was a separate chamber in the temple.

The *Tithe for the Feasts*

When God gave the law to Moses and all of the people, He also commanded that 3 times a year every male Jew was to attend a *Holy Convocation in Jerusalem*. There are three annual feasts that all males of Israel were required to attend in Jerusalem: *Passover, Shavuot* (Pentecost) and *Sukkot* (Feast of Tabernacles). Passover and Pentecost were both spring feasts, and Tabernacles was a fall feast.

The Feast of Passover (Nisan 14) is linked to the Feast of Pentecost by the Feast of Unleavened Bread (Nisan 15-Nisan 21) by the Feast of Firstfruits, which is always observed on the only Sunday which falls within the 7-day Feast of Unleavened Bread (Nisan 15-Nisan 21) on the Jewish calendar. The Feast of Pentecost is always held on the 50th day following the Feast of Firstfruits. As time went by, the entire period of time between the Feast of Passover (Nisan 14) and the Feast of Pentecost would become known as *Pentecost*.

It is obvious that every male in Jerusalem could spend a lot of time attending the 3 required Feasts of Israel. Imagine the males in each household having to leave their crops and herds 3 times a year. Males would also come from every corner of the known world and travel to and from Jerusalem. No work would be done at home unless it was by women, children or indentured servants. If not planned carefully; crops, flocks and herds of cattle could suffer greatly. God recognized this hardship and commanded that a tithe of 10% be paid in the second and sixth year of a 7-year cycle. This 7-year cycle was known since the time of Moses and was called a *Sabbatical Cycle*. The Sabbatical Cycle was patterned after the 7-day Jewish week, during which the 7th day of the week was to be a Holy Sabbath Day. The 7th year of a 7-year cycle was called a *Sabbatical year*. During a Sabbatical year, the land must rest and not be planted, tilled or harvested….it was to remain *fallow*. The purpose of the *Tithe of the Feasts* can now be explained and understood. The Tithe of the Feasts was a tithe that was to be set aside for attending the 3 required Feasts of Israel every year. This tithe is unique, because the tithe itself was not to be kept in the Tabernacle storehouse. It was to be set aside and managed by each Jewish male. It is interesting that this money could be spent in any way ……. Even partying, drinking wine and eating was allowed during the 3 required feasts. It appears from Biblical and secular records that the Jews never actually observed a Sabbatical cycle. This was the reason that the tribe of Judah was taken into Babylonian captivity for 70 years. One year for every sabbatical year that was not observed (A 490-year period of disobedience).

The *Tithe for the Poor*

Jesus Christ always related to the poor and strangers. The concern of God was so great in the Old Covenant that He ordained and commanded the Children of Israel to set aside an additional 10% every 3rd and 6th year in a 7-year sabbatical cycle to be given to the poor and strangers. It became known as the *Tithe for the Poor* or the *Maasar Ani*.

The 7th year of every Sabbatical Cycle was one in which: (1) No crops were to be sown or harvested (2) Grapes were not to be picked or pruned (Leviticus 25: 1-7). If it was against the Law of Moses (God's Law) to sow or reap, how were the people to be fed? The Lord would provide just as He had provided manna and quail to the Israelites during the 40-year Exodus. The land would yield enough food in the 6th year to sustain the people through the 7th year through planting in the 8th year until harvest in the 9th year (Leviticus 25: 20-22).

It is not hard to realize that a simple 10% tithe each year is an oversimplification of what was required by God of each Jewish male over a repeating 7-year cycle. According to the Law and the commands of God, the average tithe per year over a 7-year sabbatical cycle is as follows, but it is not specifically stated in the scriptures.

$(10\% * 5)//7 + (10\% * 7)/7 + (10\% * 2)/7 = (140\%/7) = 20\%$ PER Year!!!

It could be as much as 22.8% per year.

$(10\% * 7)/7 + (10\% * 7)/7 + (10\% * 2)/7 = 22.88\%$ per year

This was the Law under the Old Covenant and may come as a surprise to over 97% of all pastors and Christians across all denominations. This was for every male Jew that lived under the Law in the Old Testament.

Tithing Under the New Covenant

A fundamental truth under the New Covenant is the atoning work that Our Lord Jesus Christ completed on the Cross of Calvary. As Christ was drawing His last breath, he said: *It is finished* (Matthew 27:46, Mark 15:34). These were His last words to the crowd. He then looked toward heaven and said: *Father, into thy hands I commit my Spirit* (Luke 23:46). What did Christ mean when he said: *It is finished*…. It must have been terribly important…....and it was.

By saying *it is finished* Jesus was signaling to the Jewish world that there was no more need for sacrifices or temples because His work brought ultimate fulfillment to what their sacrificial system foreshadowed. When Christ died, a new and better covenant replaced the old. By saying *it is finished* Christ was saying that: My life here on earth is finished. By saying *it is finished*, Christ affirmed that the Old Covenant was finished because it was imperfect. No man could attain eternal life under the Law because no one could ever live a sinless life under the law except Jesus Christ. Even at birth, every descendent of Adam is cursed by Adam's original sin and it is imputed to us all. Christ was the perfect and pure Passover sacrificial Lamb, and he was accepted by God as an atoning sacrifice for all sins…. past, present and future. When he said *it is finished*, He declared that the entire Levitical priesthood had finished their work of offering temporary sacrifices for sin day after day, year after year. When He said *it is finished*, he declared that the barrier between His Father and the people had been removed. In the Old Testament, the only person who could directly approach God was the High Priest…....and then only once a year on the *Day of Atonement* when he went behind the veil and spoke to God, as God hovered over the Mercy Seat. In the current Dispensation of Grace, every New Covenant believer who has been born-again is allowed to directly access God through his son Jesus Christ. This was signified as Christ died by a great earthquake which rocked the temple, and tore the massive veil which separated the Hoy Place from the Holy of Holies from top to bottom. When he said that *it is finished*, he meant the Old Testament tithing system which averaged 22.86% per year over a 7-year sabbatical cycle was finished. When He said that *it is finished*, He meant the Baptism of John in the River Jordan for repentance had announced that redemption was near had been accomplished. **Praise God forever**…. The curse of the Law was finished and a new and better way had been ratified: Salvation was from that point forward and all the way back to Adam based upon *faith* and *grace*. All Old Testament saints were saved in *exactly* the same way that all New Covenant saints are saved…....by faith and by the grace of God. Those in the Old Testament were saved by the Faith of Abraham. They knew that the Law could not save anyone, and they died in faith that a Messiah would arise that would be sent by God to redeem them from sin. They did not know that Jesus Christ would be their promised redeemer, but about 75 Old Testament prophecies were fulfilled by Christ. There is no excuse for their disbelief at all. John the Baptist said it clearly when he saw Christ approaching him while he baptized Jews to repentance in the river Jordan.

The next day John saw Jesus coming unto him, and said: Behold the Lamb of God, which taketh away the sin of the world   John 1:29

Tithing in a New covenant church is something which is constantly preached. It is almost certain that before many services have come and gone, that the following passage from Malachi will be read.

[8] *Will a man rob God? Yet ye have robbed me. But ye say, wherein have we robbed thee? In tithes and offerings.*
[9] *Ye are cursed with a curse: for ye have robbed me, even this whole nation.*
[10] *Bring ye all the tithes into the storehouse, that there may be meat in mine house, and prove me now herewith, saith the LORD of hosts, if I will not open you the windows of heaven, and pour you out a blessing, that there shall not be room enough to receive it*   Malachi 3: 8-10

One of the things that cannot be done if truth is to be found in the Holy Bible is to isolate verses and interpret them out of context. Always ask the following three questions:

    Who said these words? .... Malachi

    Who is Malachi speaking to? ....Israel and the Jews

    What was the context? .... Malachi was the last prophet to

speak in the Old Testament. He was speaking to the Nation of Israel and to the Jews. In fact, he spoke 400 years before Jesus Christ would arise. The period of time between when Malachi spoke to Israel and Jesus is called the *intertestamental period*. This time is called the *400 Silent Years* because it was a span of time during which God sent no new prophets to Israel and God revealed nothing new to His people. Over 400 years later the apostle Paul would reveal the *mystery* of the church Age, which was that salvation had come to Jews and Gentiles alike…by faith and grace. So, what was Malachi saying?

Malachi asked this question to the Jews…. *not* to the Gentiles:

Will a man rob God? Yet ye have robbed me. But ye say, wherein have we robbed thee? In tithes and offerings.   Malachi 3: 8

It is very clear that Malachi is accusing the *Jews* of robbing God by not bringing their tithes and offerings into the *storehouse*. Malachi is specifically referring to the first type of a 10% tithe to the *Levites*, and the storehouse is in Solomon's Temple. But, look what Malachi says next.

[9] Ye are cursed with a curse: for ye have robbed me, even this whole nation.
[10] Bring ye all the tithes into the storehouse, that there may be meat in mine house, and prove me now herewith, saith the LORD of hosts, if I will not open you the windows of heaven, and pour you out a blessing, that there shall not be room enough to receive it.
[11] And I will rebuke the devourer for your sakes, and he shall not destroy the fruits of your ground; neither shall your vine cast her fruit before the time in the field, saith the LORD of hosts.   Malachi 3:11-12

Malachi then pleads with Israel to repent (what did John baptizer do 400 years later?). *Bring Me the tithes into My house* (the temple) as I have commanded you (in the law) and I will: *pour you out a blessing, that there shall not be room enough to receive it*. How many times have you heard a preacher say that if you will tithe 10% you will be blessed beyond measure. These words which were spoken by Malachi have NOTHING TO DO WITH THE NEW COVENANT. How many times have you heard a preacher stop at Malachi 3:8?

What is happening in Israel today? Who is on the Temple Mount? These are prophetic words spoken by Malachi and they are referring to when *Israel* will finally accept Jesus Christ as their savior (corporately) …... *all Israel will be saved* (Romans 11:26) …and the Millennial Kingdom will begin. Rightly dividing and understanding the words of Malachi is what Paul meant when he wrote:

Study to shew thyself approved unto God, a workman that needs not to be ashamed, rightly dividing the word of truth.   II Timothy 2:15

Let us examine the gospels of Matthew-Mark-Luke and John and again ask the following questions.

Who said these words?

The four Synoptic gospels are Matthew, Mark, Luke and John. Although not certain, the Gospel of Mark was probably written first, followed by Matthew and Luke in close proximity to one another, and finally the Gospel of John. They are all parallel accounts of the earthly Ministry of Jesus Christ.

To Whom are they speaking?

All four Books were written to record events which took place during the 3.5-year earthly ministry of Jesus Christ. There is a great deal of common events, but each of the 4 written accounts contain information unique to each Gospel. It is extremely important to ask:

To whom are the 4 Gospels written?

It may come as a great surprise to many, but each of the 4 synoptic gospels were a record of the earthly ministry of Jesus Christ to the *Jews,* and only the *Jews*. In fact, Jesus Christ *commanded* his 12 disciples to preach and teach only to the Jews (Matthew 10:5). *Are you a Jew or a Gentile?* Chances are, except for a few Jewish converts (a remnant) the Body of Christ today and the Church today are all Gentiles. Should this come as a surprise? …. NO. During these 3.5 years before the Cross no one knew that salvation was to be offered to Jews and Gentiles alike by faith and grace. This was a *mystery* completely unknown until the Apostle Paul wrote his 13 epistles to the Church.

And to make all men see what is the fellowship of the **mystery***, which from the beginning of the world hath been hid in God, who created all things by Jesus Christ*   Ephesians 3:9

Even the **mystery** *which hath been hid from Ages and from generations, but now is made manifest to his saints*   Colossians 1:26

What Did Paul say about Tithing?

It is interesting that Paul never said anything about a required New Covenant tithe, and yet he was chosen by God to reveal to Jews and Gentiles alike the *mystery* of salvation by faith and Grace that had replaced the Old Covenant…... NOT ONE WORD. In fact, if we survey the New Testament, we'll find that it does not prescribe a formal method or fixed amount for believers' giving at all.

Paul only indirectly referred to a required tithe in all of His epistles to the New Covenant church. The first is in Paul's letter to the Church at Corinth.

[1] *Now concerning the collection for the saints, as I have given order to the churches of Galatia, even so do ye.*
[2] *Upon the first day of the week let every one of you lay by him in store, as God*

hath prospered him, that there be no gatherings when I come
I Corinthians 16: 1-2

This has nothing to do with a new commandment for New Covenant believers to tithe. Paul is asking both churches in Galatia and Corinth to *lay aside* (collect) a sum of money to support his ministry so that he will not have to ask these churches for support when he comes to them. I Corinthians 16: 2-4 has absolutely nothing to do with New Covenant tithing. Paul is not demanding that this be done, but he is asking them to do it out of love.

In the general area of required tithing, Paul never spoke a single word. He never taught mandatory tithing of any mount, but he did teach that God loves a cheerful giver.

[6] But this I say, He which soweth sparingly shall reap also sparingly; and he which soweth bountifully shall reap also bountifully.
[7] Every man according as he purposes in his heart, so let him give; not grudgingly, or of necessity: for God loveth a cheerful giver.
[8] And God is able to make all grace abound toward you; that ye, always having all sufficiency in all things, may abound to every good work
II Corinthians 9: 6-8

And whatsoever ye do, do it heartily, as to the Lord, and not unto men
Colossians 32:23

It is interesting that Paul encouraged New Testament Christians to be a *cheerful giver*. This includes giving to the Church and other organizations which promote Jesus Christ in proportion to what he/she has been given. II Corinthians 9:6 relates to the principle of sowing and reaping which anyone could understand. If one plants a field and sows sparingly, he will reap sparingly. If one sows bountifully, he will reap bountifully. However, one should never give out of necessity and never give if it punishes your family or children.

But if any provide not for his own, and especially for those of his own house, he hath denied the faith, and is worse than an infidel   I Timothy 5:8

When one is married and has children, Paul teaches that it is a responsibility of the man in the family to provide food, clothing and the basic necessities of life to his family. The ability to stay single and serve God apart from marriage is a gift. Paul had this gift, but not everyone (I Corinthians 1: 1-9). Paul specifically admonishes

Christians to help support and sustain poor and destitute widows (I Timothy 5:16). He teaches that all Christians ought to provide for those who were less fortunate than them, and that if they did not do this, they are *worse than an infidel* (I Timothy 5:8). Those who fail to support their own families or those who are destitute and need support are said to have *denied the faith*. Christ commands us to love one another as he loved us. It is often taught in the pulpit today that a basic 10% of the gross income should be given to the offering plate according to God's command, and that any other support of a family, the poor and destitute or other religious programs would be expected based upon basic needs, and that if a person follows this command, then he/she will be blessed beyond any natural understanding. Both concepts were not taught by Paul and are not scriptural. Paul always taught that tithing is not required to be 10%......he never taught such a thing and he never preached such a thing. The Lord *loves a cheerful giver* and to give back to God a portion of the increase is both expected and is scriptural under the New Covenant. To deny your own wife and children meat and bread to give a monthly tithe of 10% is wrong.

Summary and Conclusions

Simply put, tithing was an Old Testament requirement under the law, but it is not a requirement for a New Covenant Christian. The key to understanding this truth is to recognize that the Bible is divided into 7 different periods of time called dispensations. A *dispensation* is simply a period of time during which God is dealing with His creation in a unique and special way. In a study of dispensations as they relate to tithing, there are two that are extremely important, and they are: (1) The Dispensation of the Law and (2) The Dispensation of Grace. One cannot take the commandments given to the people of God in one dispensation and apply it to another dispensation. The failure of most Christians today is a failure to rightly divide the word of God to determine what is required of a New Covenant Christian.

Study to shew thyself approved unto God, a workman that needs not to be ashamed, rightly dividing the word of truth   II Timothy 2:15

All scripture is given by inspiration of God, and is profitable for doctrine, for reproof, for correction, for instruction in righteousness: II Timothy 3:16

A primary failure in dividing the word of truth is to understand that during the 3.5-year ministry of Christ He (and His apostles) were speaking to the Jews (Matthew 10:5). The New Covenant Age of Grace was not known to Jews or Gentiles before the Apostle Paul was chosen by God on the Road to Damascus to be His chosen vessel to reveal *mysteries* previously unknown to Old Testament prophets (I Corinthians 2:7, Ephesians 1:9, Ephesians 3: 3-4, Ephesians 3:9, Colossians 1: 26-27). If the Apostle Paul was told to teach that tithing was required under The New Covenant, he certainly never said so. In fact, God made it clear in speaking through Paul that Christ had abolished the law and the curse of the law when He said *it is finished*.

The question for Christians today is: Is tithing *required* today. The answer is, NO. Is tithing a good thing and should every Christian tithe? The answer is YES and NO. Christians today should tithe a certain amount of what God has given them, but in joy…... not in response to any law or command. If any Christian does tithe, it should not be out of bondage or necessity because God loves a *cheerful giver*. It is certainly true that all of the things in this world belong to God, and He will bless anyone according to His good will and pleasure…....but not as an incentive or reward for mandatory tithing. This was not true under the Old Covenant. No individual should tithe if it is hurting his family and depriving his children when he does so. Romans 3 clearly teaches this truth.

But if any provide not for his own, and especially for those of his own house, he hath denied the faith, and is **worse** *than an infidel*   II Timothy 5:8

So how much should a Christian tithe today and how often? Tithing of one's increase should not be a constant amount, but proportional to what God has given to them between one point in time and another. If that person is struggling to support His family and tithes because it is required, he is *worse than an infidel*. These are strong words.

If one should choose to tithe from their own free will, it will be voluntary. You absolutely do not have to tithe. God will still love you just as much whether you tithe or not. *Should you then tithe if not required?* Absolutely, money is the answer to everything in the world today (except the Gift of eternal life by our lord Jesus Christ. However, you were bought with a price and that price was enormous). If you do not believe this truth, try buying groceries for your family without money…. Try to financially help the poor and strangers without money…. Or try to keep any church in existence without any money. Money is not evil; it is the love of money that is evil. Should a Christian give to his/her local church?……Absolutely.

I can testify that because of grace, God has rewarded me beyond what I might have imagined when I was a child. I tithe and I always have…and I use a 10 % tithe. I give to my local church, but not out of necessity. Although it was before the law, if a 10% tithe was given of free will from Abraham to Melchizedek……that is good enough for me. I also give willingly to other causes out of free will…. I call these *love offerings*.

Chapter 4

The Holy Spirit

The Holy Spirit and the role which it plays in the New Covenant is a topic which is often preached in the pulpit today….and it should. A Christian should not feel uncomfortable accepting that the Holy Spirit is a part of their social and religious life. Orthodox Christianity has affirmed since the earliest days of church history that the Spirit is one with the Father and Son, and co-equal in the Godhead. The Bible declares that the Holy Spirit is *the power of God* (2 Timothy 1:7); that it *leads us into all truth* (John 14:17, 26); that it enables us to *discern Spiritual things* (1 Corinthians 2:11, 14); that it is our *guarantee (seal) of eternal life* (Ephesians 1:13-14); and that *without* it we are *not His* (Romans 8:9. The average Christian is casually aware of how the Holy Spirit is present in every born-again believer, but fails to understand the real power which is given to us through the Holy Spirit. It is almost universally recognized that the Holy Spirit has been active in God's plan for mankind throughout the Old Testament, but when pressed to give examples of the work of the Holy Spirit under the Old Covenant, most saints will not be able to do so. This chapter will explain how the Holy Spirit was very much active in the Old Testament in each dispensation. The important role of the Holy Spirit in the lives of New Testament believers will then be discussed.

The Holy Spirit in the Old Testament

It is difficult to compare the Holy Spirit in the Old Testament to the Holy Spirit in the New Testament, because that term is only used twice in the Old Testament.

*Cast me not away from thy presence; and take not thy **Holy Spirit** from me*
Psalms 51:11

[10] *But they rebelled, and vexed his Holy Spirit: therefore, he was turned to be their enemy, and he fought against them.*
[11] *Then he remembered the days of old, Moses, and his people, saying: Where is he that brought them up out of the sea with the shepherd of his flock? where is he that put his **Holy Spirit** within him?*   Isaiah 63:10-11

The first is interesting, because it implies that King David did have the Holy Spirit but it could be removed by God. The second instance was by Isaiah, who is speaking about Moses when he raised his hands in faith while God parted the Red Sea. Christ will provide path to redemption for a remnant of Jews, even though the

Jewish religious system rejected Him at the Crucifixion. He will remember the days of old and Moses His servant who had the Holy Spirit within Him. In the Old Testament, even though it is rare to find the term *Holy Spirit;* it is also the "Spirit of the Lord" or the "Spirit of God", and it is likely that these two terms refer to the Holy Spirit. Proceeding with caution, we will treat these three terms the same and depending upon context will assume they are referring to the third part of the trinity. The first occurrence of the Holy Spirit seems to be in Genesis 1 when the world was created.

And the earth was without form, and void; and darkness was upon the face of the deep. And the Spirit of God moved upon the face of the waters. And *God said....*
Genesis 1: 2-17

Genesis 1 seems to indicate that the Holy Spirit was not the *Agent* of creation (God was), but He certainly was there when the world was created (Genesis 1:26).

As we try to find particular actions in the Old Testament in which the Holy Spirit is involved, it seems that the Spirit was given to particular people at particular times to execute the will of God…particularly to defeat the enemies of Israel: For example, Gideon (Judges 6:34), Sampson in Judges 5:14, and King David when he was anointed King (I Samuel 16:13). The prophet Joel prophesied and spoke of the Holy Spirit falling upon redeemed Jews on the Day of Pentecost in Jerusalem (Joel 2, Acts 2: 1-16).

[28] *And it shall come to pass afterward, that I will pour out my Spirit upon all flesh; and your sons and your daughters shall prophesy, your old men shall dream dreams, your young men shall see visions:*
[29] *And also upon the servants and upon the handmaids in those days will I pour out my Spirit* Joel 2: 28-29

Genesis 6:3 suggests that the Holy Spirit in the Old Testament was also given to certain people with a Holy calling to boldly rebuke sin. The prophet Micah condemned the house of Jacob and the nation of Israel for their sins against God. Micah admonished evil and declared the righteousness of God, and he attributed his boldness to the Spirit of the Lord (Micah 3:8). Micah said the Spirit filled him with *justice and might.*

Isaiah prophesied about Israel's coming Messiah, noting that the Spirit would rest upon Him (Isaiah 42:1). The Holy Spirit was a powerful presence from the time of creation and throughout the history of Israel, right up to the coming of Jesus Christ.

It seems that both Jesus Christ and the Holy Spirit were appointed by the Father to play important and key roles in the New Testament. Jesus Christ brought life and salvation to every new Covenant believer, while the Holy Spirit empowered every believer with gifts and power.

The Holy Spirit in the New Testament

The Holy Bible in the New Testament has much to say about the role of the Holy Spirit in a true believer's life. Any Christian will recognize the rightful place of the Holy Spirit as a member of the eternal triad of God the Father, Jesus Christ the Son and the Holy Spirit. We will characterize and explain the Holy Spirit within every New Covenant believer under 3 broad categories: (1) The *Prescence* of the Holy Spirit in every believer (2) The *Purpose* of the Holy Spirit in every born-again Christian and (3) The *Power* of the Holy Spirit.

The *Prescence* of the Holy Spirit

When Christ spoke to His apostles just before He was arrested and crucified, he told them the following:

[7] Nevertheless I tell you the truth; It is expedient for you that I go away: for if I go not away, the Comforter will not come unto you; but if I depart, I will send him unto you.
[8] And when he is come, he will reprove the world of sin, and of righteousness, and of judgment:
[9] Of sin, because they believe not on me;
[10] Of righteousness, because I go to my Father, and ye see me no more;
[11] Of judgment, because the prince of this world is judged.
[12] I have yet many things to say unto you, but ye cannot bear them now.
[13] Howbeit when he, the Spirit of truth, is come, he will guide you into all truth: for he shall not speak of himself; but whatsoever he shall hear, that shall he speak: and he will shew you things to come.
[14] He shall glorify me: for he shall receive of mine, and shall shew it unto you
John 16: 7-14

Jesus Christ promised His disciples that He would not leave them helpless, but that after He is gone, He would send them the great *comforter*, which is another term for the *Holy Spirit*. This first happened to Jewish born-again believers on the *Day of Pentecost*, when the Holy Spirit fell upon each apostle, and 3000 other Jews who had gathered in Jerusalem. After salvation was offered first to the Jews, Jesus turned to the Gentiles and anointed Paul to reveal the *mystery* of the New Covenant.

Jesus promised the Spirit as a permanent guide, teacher, seal of salvation, and comforter for believers (John 14:16-18). He also promised that the Holy Spirit's power would help His followers to spread the message of the gospel around the world: *But you will receive power when the Holy Spirit comes on you; and you will be my witnesses in Jerusalem, and in all Judea and Samaria, and to the ends of the earth* (Acts 1:8). The salvation of souls is a supernatural work only made possible by the Holy Spirit's power at work in the world.

The Holy Spirit is *omnipresent*. King David acknowledged this when he asked:

[7] *Whither shall I go from thy spirit? or whither shall I flee from thy presence?*
[8] *If I ascend up into heaven, thou art there: if I make my bed in hell, behold, thou art there.*
[9] *If I take the wings of the morning, and dwell in the uttermost parts of the sea*
Psalms 139: 7-9

This is possible because, unlike humans, the Holy Spirit is not flesh and blood but a *Spirit*. Although not often recognized, the Holy Spirit conceived Jesus Christ. We rarely consider the profound implications of Matthew 1:

Now the birth of Jesus Christ was on this wise: When as his mother Mary was espoused to Joseph, before they came together, she was found with **child of the Holy Ghost.** *Jesus Christ is the Son of God because* **He was conceived by the Holy Spirit** *of God rather than by a human father*   Matthew 1:18

It was part of God's eternal plan to send Jesus Christ to earth to redeem Israel, and also to initiate the New Covenant by which both Jews and Gentiles are saved by faith and grace. This could never have happened without the presence of the Holy Spirit in mother Mary's life. Jesus, like every other man or woman who would be born from the seed of Adam, would have been cursed by the original sin of Adam if born through normal intercourse. By being conceived through a supernatural process, Jesus Christ was born sinless and lived a sonless life under the Law. He was the only person born of woman who could redeem the entire world from all sins. He was the perfect Lamb of God who was accepted as the last and complete sacrifice for sin.

The Holy spirit helps us understand all things; He *guides us* when we need discernment and wisdom; He *leads us* when we need to discern right from wrong and He *convicts* us when we need to reject sinful acts. The Holy Spirit *reveals* to us God's truth, and God's truth *renews our conscience*.

He will give you another Helper, that He may be with you forever   John 14:16

[10] *But God hath revealed them unto us by his Spirit: for the Spirit searches all things, yea, the deep things of God.*
[11] *For what man knoweth the things of a man, save the spirit of man which is in him? even so the things of God knoweth no man, but the Spirit of God.*
[12] *Now we have received, not the spirit of the world, but the spirit which is of God; that we might know the things that are freely given to us of God.*
[13] *Which things also we speak, not in the words which man's wisdom teaches, but which the Holy Ghost teaches; comparing spiritual things with spiritual*
I Corinthians 2: 10-13

The *Purpose* of the Holy Spirit

As a part of the New Covenant, the Holy Spirit is promised to everyone who becomes a born-again Christian. There are several specific Spiritual transformations which take place when each individual decides to give their life to Jesus Christ.

(1) The word is *received*
(2) The word is *believed.*
(3) The person that truly believes and gives their life to Jesus Christ is *born again.*

The Phrase *born again* is first used by Christ in John 3. A ruler of the Jews called Nicodemus had evidently heard the gospel message, received it and wanted to believe. He came to Jesus by night and spoke:

Rabbi, we know that thou art a teacher come from God: for no man can do these miracles that thou doest, except God be with him   John 3:2

Jesus Christ, knowing the true thoughts and heart of all men, perceived that the man wanted to accept Him as the Son of God and his redeemer He responded:

Verily, verily, I say unto thee: **Except a man be born again**, *he cannot see the Kingdom of God*   John 3:3

This must have startled and confused Nicodemus because he then asked:

How can a man be born when he is old? can he enter the second time into his mother's womb, and be born? John 3:4

Jesus then told Nicodemus:

[6] *That which is born of the flesh is flesh; and that which is born of the Spirit is Spirit.*
[7] *Marvel not that I said unto thee,* **Ye must be born again**.
[8] *The wind blows where it will, and you hear the sound, but cannot tell whence it cometh, and whither it goeth: so is every one that is born of the Spirit.*
[9] *Nicodemus answered and said unto him, How can these things be?*
[10] *Jesus answered and said unto him, Art thou a master of Israel, and knowest not these things?* John 3: 8-10

Jesus rebuked Nicodemus and told him: *You are a ruler of the Jews and do not know these things?* Nicodemus had previously asked; *How can these things be?* Jesus had already revealed the truth of how He responded to Nicodemus.

[12] *But as many as received him, to them he gave power to become the sons of God, even to them that believe on his name*:
[13] *Which were born, not of blood, nor of the will of the flesh, nor of the will of man, but of God.* John 1: 12-13

The phrase *born again* means to be reborn *Spiritually*. Nicodemus needed a change in his heart…... a Spiritual transformation. ……a new birth into a new creature who is conformed to the image and will of Jesus Christ; not his own. Being born again, is an act of God whereby eternal life is imparted to the person who believes (2 Corinthians 5:17; Titus 3:5; 1 Peter 1:3; 1 John 2:29; 3:9; 4:7; 5:1-4, 18). John 1:12, 13). Being born again also involves becoming a Son of God by trusting in the name of Jesus Christ. How does this transformation take place?

The Agent by which a person is born again is by the *Holy Spirit.* Once a person believes and accepts Jesus Christ as their Lord and Savior, they immediately receive the gift of the Holy Spirit from Jesus Christ. It is by and through the Holy Spirit that a person is *baptized into the body of Christ.* Paul explained this when he revealed the *mystery* of the New Covenant.

For by one Spirit are we all baptized into one body, whether we be Jews or Gentiles, whether we be bond or free; and have been all made to drink into one Spirit   I Corinthians 12:13

For as many of you as have been baptized into Christ have put on Christ Galatians 3:27

> Baptism of the Holy Spirit can be defined as that work whereby the Spirit of God places the believer into union with Christ, and into a common Spiritual body with other believers at the moment of salvation. The baptism of the Holy Spirit was predicted by John the Baptist (Mark 1:8) and by Jesus before He ascended to heaven: *For John baptized with water, but in a few days you will be baptized with the Holy Spirit* (Acts 1:5). This promise was fulfilled on the Day of Pentecost (Acts 2: 1–4) where for the first time, people were permanently indwelt by the Holy Spirit. Being in the *body of Christ* means that we are risen with Him to newness of life (Romans 6:4). We should then exercise our Spiritual gifts to keep the body of Christ functioning properly.   Taken from *Got questions?*

The *Power* of the Holy Spirit

Paul had this to say….

For our gospel came not unto you in word only, but also in power, and in the Holy Ghost, and in much assurance; as ye know what manner of men we were among you for your sake   I Thessalonians 1:5

The *Holy Spirit* is not only the Spiritual vehicle by which every true Christian is baptized into the Body of Christ, He also permanently resides in everyone who has been born again and imparts two things into every true believer: (1) *Gifts* of the Holy Spirit and (2) *Fruits* of the Holy Spirit.

Gifts of the Holy Spirit in Old Testament

There are 7 gifts of the Holy Spirit. These 7 gifts are recognized by the Roman Catholic Church based upon Isaiah 11:2.

[1] *And there shall come forth a rod out of the stem of Jesse, and a Branch shall grow out of his roots:*
[2] *And the Spirit of the LORD shall rest upon him, the Spirit of wisdom and*

understanding, the Spirit of counsel and might, the Spirit of knowledge and of the fear of the LORD   Isaiah 11: 1-2

The Isaiah prophecy is Messianic, and actually only lists 6 gifts: (1) Wisdom (2) Understanding, (3) Counsel (4) Strength ((5) Knowledge and (6) Fear of the Lord. The Roman catholic Church later added a seventh gift; *piety*. This was done to achieve the symbolic number for completeness, which is the number **seven**. Jesus was blessed with these gifts by his Father, and those who are born-again believers will receive Holy Spirit from Jesus Christ and are blessed with these gifts by the Holy Spirit. They supply the Spiritual power and strength a person needs to accomplish his or her calling in Jesus Christ

> (1) *Wisdom*- Wisdom is the ability to distinguish right from wrong and to make logical and informed decisions. A wise man will hear and read the Holy Word of God, and increase his/her knowledge of the scriptures.
>
> *A man of discernment shall attain unto wise counsel*   Proverbs 1:5
>
> (2) *Understanding*-Understanding is the ability to discern right from wrong
>
> *The fear of the LORD is the beginning of wisdom: all who follow after Christ have good understanding*   Psalms 111:10
>
> (3) *Counsel* -Counsel is the ability to receive or give sound advice based upon God's word
>
> *A wise man will hear, and will increase learning; and a man of understanding shall attain unto wise counsel*   Proverbs 1:5
>
> (4) *Might*- Some common synonyms of might are *energy, force, power, and strength*. Might implies great or overwhelming power or strength.

Who can utter the mighty acts of the LORD? who can shew forth all his praise?   Psalms 106:2

> (5) *Knowledge*- Knowledge is the ability to study and learn; to acquire, retain and master facts and information; and use what is learned to declare that Jesus Christ is Lord and Savior

> *The heart of the prudent obtains knowledge; and the ear of the wise seeks to hear knowledge*　　Psalms 18:15

- (6) *Fear of the Lord-* Fear of the Lord is awe, reverence and respect for God. It acknowledges that everything comes as a gift from God, downplays personal achievement and self-sufficiency, and gladly offers praise, worship and adoration to God.

> *If ye will fear the LORD, and serve him, and obey his voice, and not rebel against the commandment of the LORD, then shall both ye and also the King that reigns over you continue following the LORD your God*
> I Samuel 12:14

Each of these gifts of the Holy spirit are also available to New Covenant believers. However, God has empowered each New Testament believer to receive a number of new gifts which the Holy Spirit will bring to each Born-again Christian.

Gifts of the Holy Spirit in New Testament

It has already been explained that the Holy Spirt operates within any born-again Christian in the New Covenant in a different way than in the Old Covenant. The apostle Paul spoke of one or more different *gifts* which are given to any true Christian when they receive Christ as their Lord and Savior. The gifts of the Holy Spirit are:

(1) Words of wisdom
(2) Words of knowledge
(3) Faith
(4) Gift of Healing
(5) Gift of performing miracles
(6) Gift of prophecy
(7) Spiritual discernment
(8) Gift of speaking in tongues
(9) Gift of interpretation of tongues

[7] But the manifestation of the Spirit is given to every man to profit withal.
[8] For to one is given by the Spirit the word of wisdom; to another the word of knowledge by the same Spirit;
[9] To another faith by the same Spirit; to another the gifts of healing by the same

Spirit;
[10] To another the working of miracles; to another prophecy; to another discerning of Spirits; to another different kinds of tongues; to another the interpretation of tongues:
[11] ***But all these worketh that one and the selfsame Spirit, dividing to*** *every man severally as he will*   *I Corinthians 12: 7-11*

It is obvious that these 9 gifts are available to every true believer, but they are not all activated in each New Covenant Christian. Just stop and think about what all 9 of these gifts from the Holy Spirit are really about. We are talking about God Almighty descending upon every true believer in the form of the 3rd person of the Godhead when they accept His Son as their Lord and Savior. God becomes a part of every new believer through the Holy Spirit, and manifests Himself through these 9 gifts. The activation and manifestation of one or more gifts of the Holy Spirit is not always automatic. They should be earnestly sought by every born-again Christian.

[14] Neglect not the gift that is in thee, which was given thee by prophecy, with the laying on of the hands of the presbytery.
[15] Meditate upon these things; give thyself wholly to them; that thy profiting may appear to all.
[16] Take heed unto thyself, and unto the doctrine; continue in them: for in doing this thou shalt both save thyself, and them that hear thee   *II Timothy 4: 14-16*

The Holy Spirit is a powerful force. Just stop and think about what all 9 of these gifts from the Holy Spirit are really about. We are talking about God Himself coming down and manifesting a part of Himself in everyone who accepts His Son as Lord and Savior. This is another *mystery* which is difficult to comprehend. God the Father, God the Son and God the Holy Spirit…....A triune Godhead which is of one mind, one accord and one in agreement of all things. The Holy Spirit has been sent by Jesus Christ to dwell inside of every true believer. The first thing that happens to any individual who has been *spiritually* born-again is that he/she becomes a new creature in Jesus Christ.

Therefore, if any man be in Christ, he is a new creature: old things are passed away; behold, all things are become new   *II Corinthians 5:17*

When one becomes a *new creature in Christ*, the old passes away and all things are made new in Jesus Christ. That person actually becomes a part of Jesus Christ and is heir to all of the promises. This miraculous change is not physical but *Spiritual*.

The apostle Paul tells us that all believers have died with Christ and no longer live for themselves. Our lives are no longer worldly and physical, but they are now spiritual. Our *death* is that of the old sin nature which was nailed to the cross with Christ. It was buried with Him, and just as He was raised up by the Father, so are we raised up to *walk in newness of life.*

[3] *Know ye not, that so many of us as were baptized into Jesus Christ were baptized into his death?*
[4] *Therefore we are buried with him by baptism into death: that like as Christ was raised up from the dead by the glory of the Father, even so we also should* **walk in newness of life.**
[5] *For if we have been planted together in the likeness of his death, we shall be also in the likeness of his resurrection:*
[6] *Knowing this, that our old man is crucified with him, that the body of sin might be destroyed, that henceforth we should not serve sin*   Romans 6: 3-6

The new person that will be raised up is what Paul refers to in 2 Corinthians 5:17 as the *new creation*. The Holy Spirit is the Agent or vehicle through which a new believer is baptized into Jesus Christ. This is not the baptism of the Old Covenant or John's baptism of repentance; but a new supernatural, *Spiritual* birth. Part of that Spiritual transformation is to receive forgiveness of all sin and become a new Adam……. The Old Adam has passed away. That is why Paul said:

What? know ye not that your body is the temple of the Holy Ghost which is in you, which ye have of God, and ye are not your own?   I Corinthians 6:19

[22] *For as in Adam all die, even so in Christ shall all be made alive.*

[45] *And so it is written: The first man Adam was made a living soul; the last Adam was made a quickening Spirit*   I Corinthians 15: 22, 45

Once this new creature in Christ accepts and activates the gifts which God gives them by the Holy Spirit, this new life in Christ manifests itself through the *Fruits of the Spirit.*

The Fruits of The Holy Spirit

The fruits of the Holy Spirit are those things that can only be found in a completely Born-Again Christian. There are also 9 Fruits of the Holy Spirit. A world of unbelievers seeks to find these 9 gifts, but they cannot be found. Only a Christian who is sure that he/she will be saved by Jesus Christ and is assured of eternal life can ever achieve its state of existence.

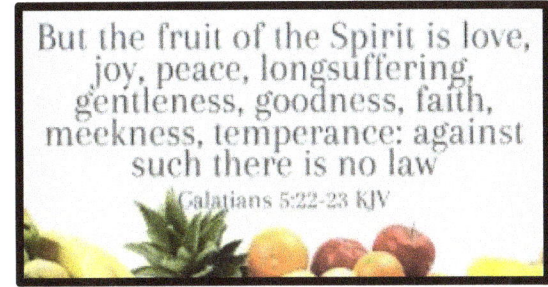

One who can go through life joined to Jesus Christ can truly find the Kingdom of God here on earth, for these things are what will be found in eternal life in a new, sinless world. This what Matthew meant when he declared:

*From that time Jesus began to preach, and to say: Repent: for the **Kingdom of Heaven** is at hand*   Matthew 4:17

We are to place all of our cares, our woes and misery upon Him. He wants us to come to Him as little children and believe that only He is *the way, the truth and the life.* Who would want to live any other way?

[16] This I say then, Walk in the Spirit, and ye shall not fulfill the lust of the flesh.
[17] For the flesh lusts against the Spirit, and the Spirit against the flesh: and these are contrary the one to the other: so that ye cannot do the things that ye would.
[18] But if ye be led of the Spirit, ye are not under the law.
[19] Now the works of the flesh are manifest, which are these; Adultery, fornication, uncleanness, lasciviousness,
[20] Idolatry, witchcraft, hatred, variance, emulations, wrath, strife, seditions, heresies,
[21] Enviers, murders, drunkenness, retellings, and such like: of the which I tell you before, as I have also told you in time past, that they which do such things shall not inherit the Kingdom of God.
*[22] **But the fruit of the Spirit is love, joy, peace, longsuffering, gentleness, goodness, faith,***
*[23] **Meekness, temperance**: against such there is no law.*
[24] And they that are Christ's have crucified the flesh with the affections and lusts.
[25] If we live in the Spirit, let us also walk in the Spirit   Galatians 5: 16-25

The average Christian does not fully understand or recognize the power which is given to each individual by the Holy Spirit. *Each Christian* is given the gift of the Holy Spirit when they accept Him as their Lord and Savior. The Holy Spirit baptizes each born-again Christian into the body of Jesus Christ, and then bestows upon that individual gifts from on high by which every Christian can function in a world of sin and unrighteousness. This is the victory that we have in Jesus Christ.

Summary

The Holy Spirit cannot be found in every person. It is a gift that is given to every Christian who is born again and has been crucified with Christ. The Bible declares that the Holy Spirit is *the power of God* (2 Timothy 1:7); that it *leads us to all truth* (John 14:17, 26); that it enables us to *discern Spiritual things* (1 Corinthians 2:11, 14); that it is our *guarantee (seal) of eternal life* (Ephesians 1:13-14); and that *without* it we are *not His* (Romans 8:9). Perhaps the most important thing that the Holy Spirit does for every born-again Christian is to baptize every true believer into Jesus Christ. The baptism of the Holy Spirit may be defined as that work whereby the Spirit of God places the believer into union with Christ and into union with other believers in the body of Christ This is a Spiritual transformation by which every true believer becomes a part of the body of Christ. As a member of the Body of Christ, one becomes an heir and joint heir to all of the promises. The apostle John said:

I knew him not: but he that sent me to baptize with water, the same said unto me: Upon whom thou shalt see the Spirit descending, and remaining on him, the same is he which baptizes with the Holy Ghost.   John 1:33

We were all baptized by one Spirit into one body   I Corinthians 12:13

For John truly baptized with water; but ye shall be baptized with the Holy Ghost not many days hence   Acts 1:5

Know ye not, that so many of us as were baptized into Jesus Christ were baptized into his death?   Romans 6:3

The Holy Spirit is that spiritual vehicle by which every true believer can join the body of Christ and enter in communion with God the Father. Without the indwelling of the Holy Spirit, the spirit man cannot communicate with God the spiritual man. God is a spirit, and spiritual things cannot understand or communicate with non-spiritual things. *Prayer* is the way in which we communicate with God who created us and saved us through His son Jesus Christ, because he desires to be in an intimate relationship with us just as He was with Adam in the Garden of Eden. God talks to us **through His word and the Holy Spirit in us**. The Holy Spirit helps us understand His word and apply it to our lives.

In the Garden of Eden, God and Adam communicated in a personal way, not through any intermediatory. Before the Law was given to Moses and the people of Israel, communication was not face to face as two men normally talk, but man would hear from God only when and how God chose to commune with man. Under the Old Covenant and the Law, common man was separated from God and could only be heard through the High Priest, or on special occasions when God or the Holy spirit came to man for special assignments and purpose. Under the New Covenant, the only communication with God was by true believers enabled by the Holy Spirit. When the Church Age ends; Man, God the Father, God the son and the Holy Spirit will co-exist for 1000 years in the Millennial Kingdom. Jesus Christ will rule over the entire world from His throne just outside the New Jerusalem on His Throne of Glory, which will sit in the New Holy Temple on a great elevated plateau. The eternal plan of God will finally be realized after the earth is purged of all sin and the eternal Kingdom of God begins. At that time, God's Great Plan for the redemption of all mankind will be completed, and God will once again commune with Man just as He did with Adam and Eve before sin entered the world and Paradise was Lost.

Fruits of the Holy Spirit

Love	Joy	Peace
Longsuffering	Gentleness	Goodness
Faith	Meekness	Temperance

Gifts of the Holy Spirit

Wisdom	Knowledge	Faith
Healing	Miracles	Prophecy
Spiritual Discernment	Speaking in Tongues	Interpreting Tongues

Chapter 5

The Genealogy of Jesus Christ: Matthew and Luke

The genealogy of Jesus Christ is given by both Matthew (Matthew 1: 1-16) and Luke (Luke 3: 23-38). At first glance, the genealogy of Matthew and of Luke seem to be contradictory. Matthew 1:16 clearly states that the father of Joseph is Jacob, and Luke 3:23 states says that the father of Joseph is Heli.

And Jacob begat Joseph the husband of Mary, of whom was born Jesus, who is called Christ   Matthew 1:16

And Jesus himself began to be about thirty years of Age, being (as was supposed) the son of Joseph, which was the son of Heli   Luke 3:23

The literal Greek rendering of Luke 3:23 is as follows.

Καὶ	αὐτὸς	ἦν	Ἰησοῦς	ἀρχόμενος	ὡσεὶ	ἐτῶν	τριάκοντα	Ὢν	υἱός	ὡς
And	Himself	was	Jesus	beginning	about	years [old]	thirty	being	son	as

ἐνομίζετο	Ἰωσὴφ	τοῦ	Ἠλὶ
was supposed	of Joseph	-	of Heli

The literal Greek to English translation of Luke 3:23 removes all difficulty.

Jesus, when He began, was about thirty years old, being the son (as it was thought) of Joseph, of Heli

This does not at all mean that Jesus was the son of Heli, but that Jesus was a descendant, on His mother's side, of Heli. The word *son* υἱός in the Greek has this dual meaning.

If we investigate the genealogy of Mary, we discover that Mary's father was Heli, and Joseph's father was a man named Jacob (Matthew 1:16). When Heli is encountered in Luke 3:23, it becomes clear that Luke is tracing the genealogy of Jesus through his actual mother, Mary…. and not through Joseph. Incidentally, when Luke 3:23 says that Joseph was the son of Heli, the words *son of* are *not* in the original Greek. These two words ae usually italicized in other translations to avoid confusion with Matthew 1:16.

The genealogy in Matthew 1 and Luke 3 are different because one traces the genealogy of Christ through His earthly father, Joseph (Matthew), and the genealogy in Luke traces the linage of Christ through His natural mother Mary. Did Joseph adopt Jesus Christ as his own son? What do the scriptures say?

[18] *Now the birth of Jesus Christ was on this wise: When as his mother Mary was espoused to Joseph, before they came together, she was found with child of the Holy Ghost.*
[19] *Then Joseph her husband, being a just man, and not willing to make her a public example, was minded to put her away privily.*
[20] *But while he thought on these things, behold, the angel of the Lord appeared unto him in a dream, saying, Joseph, thou son of David, fear not to take unto thee Mary thy wife: for that which is conceived in her is of the Holy Ghost.*
[21] *And she shall bring forth a son, and thou shalt call his name JESUS: for he shall save his people from their sins.*
[22] *Now all this was done, that it might be fulfilled which was spoken of the Lord by the prophet, saying,*
[23] *Behold, a virgin shall be with child, and shall bring forth a son, and they shall call his name Emmanuel, which being interpreted is, God with us.*
[24] *Joseph being raised from sleep did as the angel of the Lord had Then bidden him, and took unto him his wife:*
[25] *And knew her not till she had brought forth her firstborn son: and he called his name JESUS*   Matthew 1: 18-25

Given the importance of linage to the Jewish tradition, it is strange that Jewish law never developed a formal legal procedure for adoption except in the case of a brother who dies and leaves a widow and children (Deuteronomy 25: 5-6). But, from this narrative we can see that Jesus was conceived supernaturally within the virgin and unmarried Mary by the Holy Ghost. Joseph took Mary legally as his wife prior to Jesus' birth, though they did not consummate the marriage until after Jesus was born.

Based upon this, it seems clear that there may not have needed to be any real formal adoption. Jesus would have been born as Joseph's son without any need for adoption since Jesus was born when Mary and Joseph were already married. It seems pretty clear that by following the divine directive of God (Matthew 1:20) and marrying Mary before Jesus was born, that Joseph accepted his place as Jesus earthly father and adopted Jesus as a son. Only Mary and Joseph would have known otherwise. We will now look at the two genealogies in more detail.

The Linage of Matthew

Matthew was a Jew and he was a tax collector. Roman tax collectors were not respected nor accepted socially among the Jews because most collected taxes, skimmed money off of the collection, and passed the rest on to Rome. There is no evidence that Matthew engaged in those practices before He was ordained by Christ to be an Apostle…but he was probably not well liked by the Jews. This is just another instance of Christ using ordinary people for extraordinary service.

In his Gospel, Matthew was always concerned with establishing Jesus Christ as King of the Jews. To inculcate Christ as King of the Jews he had to document and establish two things: (1) Jesus had to come from the Tribe of Judah (2) Jesus Christ must come from the royal Davidic Line. Hence, a central theme of this genealogy and one that runs throughout the Gospel of Matthew was that Jesus Christ was the prophesied Jewish Messiah; that He was the Son of God; and that he was qualified to sit upon the throne of David as King. After the Church Age comes to an end, Jesus would rule and reign over the Jews both during the 1000-year Millennial Kingdom and during the eternal Kingdom of God. The genealogy of Matthew traces the linage of Christ back to King David and Abraham to establish His right to do so.

It is interesting that Matthew broke with Jewish tradition in two significant ways: (1) He included women in His genealogy ……Tamar, Rahab, Ruth, and Bathsheba. (2) He included Gentiles. The 1st was Tamar. She was widowed twice, and the fourth son of Jacob called Judah was eventually responsible to care for her. By Jewish law, when a brother died and his wife was widowed, the remaining brother was supposed to take her in marriage and sire children with her on his brother's behalf. Judah refused to father children with her, and when Judah's first wife died Tamar disguised herself as a harlot and seduced Judah. Their union resulted in her giving birth to twin boy, and in a complicated story forced Judah into accepting her as his wife. Hence, she became a part of the Davidic line. Tamar and Judah later bore twin boys named Perez and Zerah (Genesis 38). Ironically, out of Perez's line, both King David and later Jesus Christ, the Messiah, were born (Matthew 1:3).

Matthew also included Rahab the Jericho harlot and Ruth who was a hated Moabite. Rahab protected a group of Jews from the enemy by hiding them in her room, and she later married Salmon of the Tribe of Judah and was the mother of Boaz.

Ruth was a Moabite and an unclean woman, but she wound up marrying Boaz. Boaz and Ruth bore a son, Obed, who became the grandfather of David and the ancestor of Jesus Christ.

This is testament to God's prevailing mercy. God can use even the most flawed and sinful of men and women for His divine purposes, not because of their merit, but because of His grace and love for others.

> The people in the line of the Messiah were not perfect people, they were fallen people, and they were sinful people. They were people who are as much in need of a Savior as anyone else, and that's part of the beauty of this genealogy in the opening section of Matthew. Jesus didn't come from this line of super people. Jesus came from a line of people that were broken and fallen, and through His perfect life, He was going to overcome all of that; all of the sin of the world, all of the broken people, all of the fallen people of the world, and He was going to become a message, a center of hope for lost people. This is a beautiful illustration of Jesus' humanity. He is incarnate, His full God nature, combining with fully human nature to become the ultimate man, fully man, fully God, perfect in every way, the only one who could ultimately accomplish the work that He accomplished
> *Another 12* Ministries website

The linage of Matthew showed that Jesus Christ was from both the loins of Abraham and was a direct descendant of King David.

The Linage of Luke

Matthew organizes Jesus' genealogy into three groups of fourteen names: Abraham to David, Solomon to Jeconiah), and Shealtiel to Jesus Christ. Luke's list runs in the opposite direction, beginning with Christ and ending with Adam, whom he calls *the son of God*. His list contains 42 men and four women, all of whom are ancestors of Jesus. As just discussed, the genealogy of Matthew was written primarily to prove to the Jews that He was descended from Abraham and King David. Luke wrote primarily to Gentiles, and he stressed the humanity of Jesus Christ throughout his book. Luke also included in his linage the names of scandalous and disreputable women, and like Matthew intended to show that Jesus Christ was the redeemer of all mankind.... not just royalty or important people. Jesus died for Jews and Gentiles alike, from all walks of life and social status.

It is estimated that Jesus fulfilled somewhere between seventy-two and three hundred prophecies. However, if you take just the minimum 72 prophecies, which is fairly agreed upon amongst believers, then it is important to understand the probability of one man fulfilling seventy-two ancient prophecies about himself. The mathematics and astronomy professor Peter W. Stoner actually said, "Let us just take eight prophecies, and look at the probability of only those 8 being fulfilled by Jesus Christ. Eight ancient prophecies being fulfilled by a man like Jesus is a chance of 1 in 10, to the 17th power. To illustrate this probability, Professor Stoner gave this example. Such a probability would be equivalent to covering the whole state of Texas with silver dollars two feet deep. Then expecting a blindfolded man to walk across the state, and, on the very first try, find the one coin that was marked beforehand. You see, God has given us evidence of Himself, and Matthew has laid out the foundation for his gospel's argument in this genealogy, and He continues to lay out the evidence for why people can confidently believe that Jesus is the Messiah, the savior of the world   Another 12 Ministries

What is the difference in the genealogy of Matthew and That of Luke?

Matthew starts with Abraham, while Luke begins with Adam. The Old Testament prophets wrote that the Messiah would come from the line of David (I Chronicles 17: 11-14). Both Matthew and Luke provide genealogies of Jesus that confirm He was a descendent of David. This had to be established because of a prophecy that Samuel wrote concerning the Throne of David.

And thine house and thy Kingdom shall be established for ever before thee: thy throne shall be established forever   II Samuel 7:16

Therefore, He (Jesus Christ) was qualified to sit upon the throne of David as King of the Jews.

The lists are identical between Abraham and David, but differ radically from that point. Matthew has twenty-seven generations from David to Joseph, whereas Luke has forty-two, with almost no overlap between the names on the two lists. But they differ in another important way: Matthew follows the line of David's son Solomon, while Luke follows the line of Nathan, another son of David. The end result is two distinct genealogies. Both Matthew and Luke present Jesus as the King of Israel by connecting Him to the line of Abraham. More importantly through the line of Mary, He was a flesh and blood descendant of King David through David's son

Nathan. Thus, Jesus had the proper credentials for the throne of David in either case.

There is a second requirement which must be satisfied to show that Jesus was the Messiah. He had to be from the Tribe of Judah, and He would be called the *Lion of Judah* (Revelation 5:5).

One of the mysteries surrounding the genealogy of Luke concerns the fact that it contains the name of *Jeconiah*. The problem lies in the historical record of the prophet Jeremiah, which reveals that no descendent of Jeconiah would ever rule upon the throne of David. (Jeremiah 22: 29-30).

[29] *O earth, earth, earth, hear the word of the LORD.*
[30] *Thus saith the LORD: Write ye this man childless, a man that shall not prosper in his days: for no man of his seed shall prosper, sitting upon the throne of David, and ruling any more in Judah.* Jeremiah 22: 29-30

If Jesus was a descendent of Jeconiah, then how could He ever reign on David's throne? How can this be resolved?

Jeconiah was the son and successor of King Jehoiakim, and the grandson of King Josiah. One solution might involve the virgin birth of Jesus Christ. Jesus had only one human parent, Mary. His mother was of David's line, but not through Jeconiah (Luke 3:31). Joseph was Jesus' legal father, but not His physical one. Thus, Jesus was of royal blood through Mary, but the curse of Jeconiah stopped with Joseph and was not passed on to Jesus.

The people in the line of the Messiah given by Luke through Mary were not perfect people, they were immoral and sinful people. They were people who needed a Savior just like every other Jew. Jesus did not descend from a line of saintly people. Jesus came from a line of people that were broken and fallen, and through His perfect life and sacrificial death he would redeem all sinners regardless of social status, piety or holiness. This is a beautiful illustration of Jesus' humanity. He was the only one who ever lived upon this earth that could save mankind and offer salvation to all.

Chapter 6

What Will Happen After Death?

All Christians look to Jesus Christ as their Lord and Savior. What does this mean to the average born-again Christian?

- Jesus Christ was born sinless of the Virgin Mary.
- He was the Son of God
- He offered Himself as the perfect, sinless Lamb of God for the sins of the world
- He was crucified, dead and buried, and He rose from the dead after 3 days and 3 nights.
- Because He was raised from the dead by the Power of God, we are promised by Jesus Christ and sealed by the Holy Spirit that we too will be raised from the dead and spend eternity with him

Jesus Christ has said that the gift of eternal life is freely given to those who believe in Him.

[25] *Jesus said: I am the resurrection, and the life: he that believeth in me, though he were dead, yet shall he live:*
[26] *And whosoever live and believeth in me shall never die.*   John 11 25-26

Man is not a body with a soul, but a soul with a body. The outward man which we call a *body* will die and go away at death, but the *soul* of man will live forever. A third part of man is known as the *Spirit*. Taken together, these 3 components are the essence of what actually constitutes a living soul.

The Threefold Composition of Man

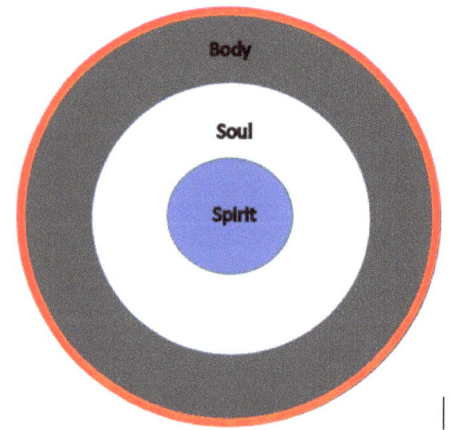

*And the very God of peace sanctify you wholly; and I pray God your whole **Spirit and soul and body** be preserved blameless unto the coming of our Lord Jesus Christ* I Thessalonians 5:23

*For the word of God is quick, and powerful, and sharper than any two-edged sword, piercing even to the dividing asunder of **soul and Spirit**, and of the joints and marrow, and is a discerner of the thoughts and intents of the heart.* Hebrews 4:12

*Fear not them which kill the body, but are not able to kill the soul: but rather fear him which is able to destroy both **soul and body** in hell* Matthew 10:28

*And the very God of peace sanctify you wholly; and I pray God your whole **spirit and soul and body** be preserved blameless unto the coming of our Lord Jesus* I Thessalonians 5:23

Man exists in 3 different persons: (1) Body (2) Soul and (3) Spirit, just as God exists in 3 different persons (1) Father (2) Son and (3) Holy Spirit. The difference is in the eternal existence of the two triumvirates. God in 3 persons has always existed, and will exist forever…. they are *eternal*. Man in three persons is *temporal*. The *body* of man at death will corrode and disappear in the earth at death (I Corinthians 15: 35-38), the *Spirit* will return to God from whence it came (Ecclesiastes 12:7), but the *soul* will live on forever either in a state of eternal bliss with God and Jesus Christ, or in a state of torment with Satan in the Lake of Burning Fire (Revelation 20: 4, 12-15). At physical death, the body and spirit will separate from the soul.

Then (at death) *shall the dust return to the earth as it was: and the Spirit shall return unto God who gave it* Ecclisiastes12:7

Within the internal man are two key organs which decide whether he will choose to follow Jesus Christ or follow Satan: The *heart* and the *mind*. The *heart* is where emotion, feelings and love all intersect. The heart is central to who a man really is and how he feels.

Once a person places his faith in Jesus Christ, God sends the Holy Spirit to regenerate, indwell, baptize, and seal the new believer. The old, dead Spirit of man is replaced by the Holy Spirit of God. The soul of believer can choose to walk in the Spirit or walk in the flesh (Galatians 5: 16-26). Sin wants to drag us to Spiritual death and physical destruction (Romans 7:24). An *unbeliever* chooses to sin and follow Satan. The prophet Jeremiah wrote that the heart is inherently evil and controls emotion, lust and deceit.

The heart is deceitful above all things, and desperately wicked: who can know it?
Jeremiah 17:9

The Apostle Mark also did not trust the heart.

[21] For from within, out of the heart of men, proceed evil thoughts, adulteries, fornications, murders,
[22] Thefts, covetousness, wickedness, deceit, lasciviousness, an evil eye, blasphemy, pride, foolishness:
[23] All these evil things come from within, and defile the man.   Mark 7: 21-23

Jesus Christ knew that wickedness resides in the heart of man and that if anyone was to follow Him, they must harness the heart.

For with the heart man believeth unto righteousness; and with the mouth confession is made unto salvation.   Romans 10:10

[36] Master, which is the great commandment in the law?
[37] Jesus said unto him: Thou shalt love the Lord thy God with all thy heart, and with all thy soul, and with all thy mind.
[38] This is the first and great commandment.
[39] And the second is like unto it: Thou shalt love thy neighbor as thyself.
[40] On these two commandments hang all the law and the prophets
Matthew 22: 36-40

Man was created by God from the dust of the earth. He was perfect in every way, but he was a lifeless form: *And the LORD God formed man out of the dust of the ground, and breathed into his nostrils the breath of life; and man became a living soul* (Genesis 2:7). It was the very breath of God that brought life into the lifeless form that God Himself had fashioned. It was the breath of God that breathed His own life into the lifeless body of Adam. The life of all living beings was originated by God (Genesis 1:20-25), but the life which characterizes man began with the personal breath of God and man became a *living Soul* (Genesis 2:8). God named the first man Adam which in Hebrew is *A'dama*.... which literally means *earth.* From the beginning, man was created to worship God in Spirit and in truth

(Exodus 31:3): *And I have filled him with the **Spirit** of God, in wisdom, and in understanding, and in knowledge, and in all manner of workmanship.* It was the same Spirit that is now given to man when he is *born again*……called the **Holy Spirit**. Man was created perfect and sinless. He walked and talked with Jesus… and everything was innocent, good and perfect. But then we know the story…Adam fell and committed the 1st sin when he ate of the fruit of the Tree of Knowledge …. which God had commanded him not to do. And so, Adam fell. When Adam sinned, it corrupted the entire human race since his seed spawned the entire human race. This is called the *original sin*.

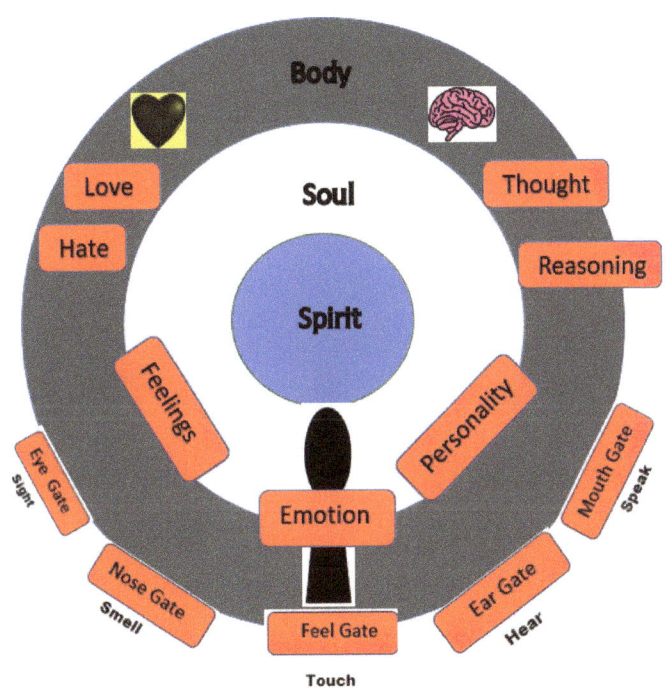

Man was made alive by God as a composite of *Body, Soul* and *Spirit*. The previous diagram shows how these three components of man work together. The Body, Soul and Spirit are separate parts but they are interrelated. The *body* of man is that part of man which interacts with the world. The *body* is man's interface to the outside world, and it is heavily influenced by all that the world might offer. The *Spirit man* is that part of man which allows every born-again Christian access to God. The human soul is that part of a person that is eternal. It is the only part of man that lives on after the body dies and decays and the spirit returns to God. Jesus said we were not to fear men, who can only kill the body, but not the soul (Matthew 10:28). Every human (male or female) is either spiritual or carnal. The *carnal man* is an unbeliever who does not possess the Holy Spirit (Romans 8: 6-7). A carnal man is also called a *natural man* in the New Testament.

A natural man is transformed into a spiritual man when they are born again. A carnal man cannot understand God nor communicate with God. They cannot know of Spiritual things because they have no Spiritual discernment.

The natural man does not receive the things of the Spirit of God: for they are foolishness unto him: neither can he know them, because they are Spiritually discerned   I Corinthians 2:14

When we define the *Spiritual* man, the *soul* is that part of man that will live forever. The unbeliever has a soul, and every true-believer has a soul. The difference is that all nonbelievers cannot communicate with God because God is *Spirit*.

*God is a **Spirit**: and they that worship him must worship him in Spirit and in truth* John 4: 24

The soul of man communicates with the body of man through several *gates* which react to what is going on in the world around us. These *gates* are: (1) the *eye gate* which tells the soul what it sees (2) The *nose gate* which tells the soul what it smells (3) The *mouth gate* which tells the lips and the vocal cords what to speak (4) The *ear gate* which tells the soul what it hears and the (5) *touch gate* which tell the soul what is being touched and grasped. The *internal body* has many organs which function in harmony.

The *Holy Spirit* is given to every born-again Christian. This same Holy Spirit is in some mysterious way a part of the triune Godhead (God the Father, God the Son and the Holy Spirit), but the *soul* of man is *who we are*. Every part of the body is crucial for survival, but if you had to rank the importance of each *physical* organ, it seems the *mind* and the *heart* would be at the top.

The Heart is one of the most important *physical* organs in the body. It is also one of the most important links to the spiritual man as well. The heart is heavily dependent upon the 5 gates which link the body to the soul, and the influence of the Holy Spirit. It is easily deceived and can wreak havoc upon even the most dedicated man of God.

The *heart* refers to that physical part of a human that controls the desires, emotions, hopes, dreams, and other intangible parts of our individuality. The *mind* typically refers to the part of a human that controls the intellect, reasoning, and thoughts.

The *mind is* predisposed to think about things which are contrary to the way God thinks and acts. This is called *carnal thinking*. When a person is born-again, God expects us to discard our carnal thinking and begins to set our mind on the things of the Spirit.

And be not conformed to this world: but be ye transformed by the renewing of your mind, that ye may prove what is that good, and acceptable, and perfect, will of God Romans 12:2

We are transformed by the *renewing of our mind* (Romans 12:2), but we are saved by *faith* (Ephesians 2:8-10). The mind and heart must both be engaged in this process because to have faith in God, we must believe and trust in God. Believing involves thoughts of the *mind*, but to trust someone requires the *heart*. Both the mind and heart usually agree and converge to a common understanding of affection, anger, love, hate and shame. The heart reflects compassion and understanding, and it is a symbol for love. The heart is heavily influenced by both affection and passion. The heart can easily overwhelm the thoughts of the mind.

The heart is deceitful above all things, and desperately wicked: who can know it? Jeremiah 17:9

The heart of a born-again Christian is one of love, joy, peace, patience, kindness, goodness, faithfulness, gentleness, self-control. A healthy heart is ruled by God's Holy Spirit and not by our flesh or our mind.

The body and Spirit of man are constantly at war with one another in a fight between good and evil. The Spirit of a believer is that part of man which communicates with God, and the Spirit of a born-again Christian is the Holy Spirit. The moment that anyone believes in Jesus Christ as their Lord and Savior, that person is sent the Holy Spirit to guide his thoughts, actions and ways. This is part of what we call being *born-again*. Jesus said:

[3] *Jesus answered and said unto him, Verily, verily, I say unto thee, Except a man be born again, he cannot see the kingdom of God.*
[4] *Nicodemus saith unto him, How can a man be born when he is old? can he enter the second time into his mother's womb, and be born?*
[5] *Jesus answered, Verily, verily, I say unto thee, Except a man be* **born of water** *and* **of the Spirit**, *he cannot enter into the kingdom of God*   John 3: 3-5

A Born-again Christians is made alive by the Holy Spirit...... Unbelievers are Spiritually dead without the Holy Spirit.

[10] But God hath revealed them unto us by his Spirit: for the Spirit searches all things, yea, the deep things of God.
[11] For what man knoweth the things of a man, save the Spirit of man which is in him? even so the things of God knoweth no man, but the Spirit of God.
[12] Now we have received, not the Spirit of the world, but the Spirit which is of God; that we might know the things that are freely given to us of God.
[13] Which things also we speak, not in the words which man's wisdom teaches, but which the Holy Ghost teaches; comparing Spiritual things with Spiritual.
[14] But the natural man receives not the things of the Spirit of God: for they are foolishness unto him: neither can he know them, because they are Spiritually discerned.   I Corinthians 2: 10-14

The body, mind and Spirit of a born-again Christian is of one accord and agrees to a common purpose: *thou shalt love the Lord thy God with all thy heart, and with all thy soul, and with all thy mind, and with all thy strength* (Mark 12:30). Led by the wisdom and discernment of the Holy Spirit; the body, mind and Spirit will collectively seek to please God and do His will. Such a person is said to be a *mature Christian* in Jesus Christ.

This brief discussion has been concerned with how both believers and unbelievers' function in this mortal life. At death, the body is placed in a grave: It decays and returns to the dust from whence it came. The Spirit of all born-again Christians returns to God from which it came. That part of man which will live forever is the *soul...... it is immortal. Where will the soul go at mortal death? How will the soul function in the afterlife and how will it be reunited with a new, sinless incorruptible body?*

The Eternal Destiny of the Soul

The battleground of emotion between good and evil is the *soul*. The soul of man can experience pain, grief and happiness. It is constantly at war with the physical man (outward body) and the inner man (Spiritual component). Forget about what pastors have said concerning these three questions and seek the answers in the Word of God.

    What did Jesus say?

[1] Let not your heart be troubled: ye believe in God, believe also in me.
[2] In my Father's house are many mansions: if it were not so, I would have told you. I go to prepare a place for you.

[3] And if I go and prepare a place for you, I will come again, and receive you unto myself; that where I am, there ye may be also.   John 14: 1-3

One should notice that Jesus told His apostles three important statements in John 14. Jesus and His 12 apostles had just finished what is known as the *Lord's Last Supper*. He astonished them by revealing that He would soon be betrayed by Judas (John 14:18). He then continued to confuse and perplex the 11 by revealing that He had been with them for over 3 years, but now He must go (John 14: 4-5).

Simon Peter said unto him, Lord, whither goest thou? Jesus answered him, Whither I go, thou canst not follow me now; but thou shalt follow me afterwards. John 13:36

Jesus said that: *Whither I go, thou cannot follow me now; but you will follow me afterwards.* If anyone is to join Jesus and the Father, he/she must be sinless in the sight of God the Father. This can only be accomplished in one way.... the Blood of Jesus cleanses us from all sin.

...if we walk in the light, as he is in the light, we have fellowship one with another, and the blood of Jesus Christ his Son cleanses us from all sin.   I John 1:7

This does not mean that we never sinned, but that by the Blood of Christ God never recognizes or sees the sin in us. When any person (Jew or Gentile) accepts Jesus Christ as their Lord and Savior, they immediately are cleansed and become a new creature in Christ. This is not when Christ will appropriate holiness, this will happen when Jesus Christ comes with all of His saints. *When is that going to take place?* At the 2nd coming of Christ. Paul revealed this to us.

.... he may stablish your hearts unblameable in holiness before God, even our Father, at the coming of our Lord Jesus Christ with all his saints
I Thessalonians 3:13

[15] For this we say unto you by the word of the Lord, that we which are alive and remain unto the coming of the Lord shall not prevent them which are asleep.
[16] For the Lord himself shall descend from heaven with a shout, with the voice of the archangel, and with the trump of God: and the dead in Christ shall rise first:
[17] Then we which are alive and remain shall be caught up together with them in the clouds, to meet the Lord in the air: and so shall we ever be with the Lord
I Thessalonians 4: 15-17

Paul wrote that at some future point in time, the Lord (Jesus Christ) will: (1) *descend from heaven*. (2) The dead in Christ will be *raised first* (3) Those who are *alive* will then rise to meet Him in the air and (4) We who are alive or dead will then *be with the Lord forever*. Has this happened yet? ….. *No*. Saints have died over the past 2000 years and they have not been resurrected or raised to join Christ. Note what else Paul had written.

[50] *Now this I say, brethren, that flesh and blood cannot inherit the Kingdom of God; neither doth corruption inherit incorruption.*
[51] *Behold, I shew you a mystery; We shall not all sleep, but we shall all be changed,*
[52] *In a moment, in the twinkling of an eye, at the last trump: for the trumpet shall sound, and the dead shall be raised incorruptible, and we shall be changed.*
[53] *For this corruptible must put on incorruption, and this mortal must put on immortality.*
[54] *So when this corruptible shall have put on incorruption, and this mortal shall have put on immortality, then shall be brought to pass the saying that is written, Death is swallowed up in victory*   I Corinthians 15: 50-54

We know that all have sinned and fallen short of the glory of God, and all have the original sin of Adam upon their mortal bodies. But corrupted and sinful bodies cannot enter the Kingdom of heaven (I Corinthians 15:50). Hence, before anyone can ascend to heaven and inherit eternal life, their mortal, sinful body must be changed and replaced: (1) Mortality must put on immortality……I Corinthians 15: 52-53 and (2) The dead must be raised with an incorruptible body …. I Corinthians 15:50. When did Jesus Christ say that He will return and gather all true believers to Him?

[29] **Immediately after the tribulation of those days** *(the Great tribulation) shall the sun be darkened, and the moon shall not give her light, and the stars shall fall from heaven, and the powers of the heavens shall be shaken:*
[30] **And then shall appear the sign of the Son of man in heaven: and then shall all the tribes of the earth mourn, and they shall see the Son of man coming in the clouds of heaven with power and great glory.**
[31] **And he shall send his angels** *with a great sound of a trumpet,* **and they shall gather together his elect** *from the four winds, from one end of heaven to the other* Matthew 24: 29-31

For we know that if our earthly house of this tabernacle were dissolved, we have a building of God, a house not made with hands, eternal in the heavens
II Corinthians 5:1

For we must all appear before the judgment seat of Christ; that every one may receive the things done in his body, according to that he hath done, whether it be good or bad   II Corinthians 5:10

All of these things will be a one-time event. *When will this take place.... At death?* **No.**

Before the transformation from an earthly body to a heavenly body can occur, Christ must return again and the earth will experience dramatic changes: *the sun be darkened, and the moon shall not give her light, and the stars shall fall from heaven.* **Then**, Christ will appear in the heavenlies to gather His ecclesia or the saints to Him (Matthew 24:31). **All** of the earth will witness this event (Matthew 24:30). The words of Christ cannot be misunderstood: these things will not take place until ***after*** *the tribulation of those days* (Matthew 24:29). What is the *tribulation of those days?* It should be perfectly clear that those days are the Great tribulation which John describes in the Book of Revelation. Note that the tribulation that will occur at the end of the Church Age is what Christ had been describing to His disciples (and us) in Matthew 24-25).

The purpose of this lengthy study of God's Word has been to show that before anyone who dies in Christ can be joined to Christ forever, the events of Matthew 24: 29-31, I Corinthians 15: 50-54 and I Thessalonians 4: 15-17 must take place, and this will not happen until the Rapture occurs. This sets the framework by which the following question must be answered: What *will happen to anyone (saint or sinner) who has died under both the Old Covenant and the New Covenant?*

What Happens at Death?

Death is an event which is almost universally misunderstood by almost every Christian. In every church that I have visited over the past 30 years, it has been preached that when a Christian dies, that person is immediately taken to heaven where they will be with Jesus Christ forever. This is impossible since there must be a dramatic transformation of each person before they can be joined to Jesus Christ forever.

There are only three dispensations of time which will be discussed. They are: (1) The Dispensation of Law…... Old Covenant (2) The Dispensation of Grace…...New Covenant and (3) The 1000-Year Millennial Kingdom

Where Does the Soul of a Person Go at Death?

As previously discussed, *every human is not a man/woman with a soul, but a soul with a body.* At death the **body** is placed in the grave, decays and dies. It is lifeless without the blood, because *life is in the blood.* The **Spirit** of a man returns to God from which it came: *Then shall the dust return to the earth as it was: and the Spirit shall return unto God who gave it* (Ecclesiastes 12:7). All men are created with a living soul which never dies, and it will live forever. *Behold, all souls are mine; as the soul of the father, so also the soul of the son is mine* (Ezekiel 18:4). The **Soul** was placed in man at the point of conception and never dies. The soul acts as a link between the material body and the Spirit man and therefore shares some characteristics of both. The soul can reason….it can think…...it can discern good from evil and it can reason and understand. In an *unbeliever*, the soul is constantly at war with the body, but it is *cut off* from the Holy Spirit and God. There is no place in Scripture that says an unbeliever has the Holy Spirit. Only believers have the Holy Spirit.

[12] *Now we have received, not the Spirit of the world, but the Spirit which is of God; that we might know the things that are freely given to us of God.*
[13] *Which things also we speak, not in the words which man's wisdom teaches, but which the Holy Ghost teaches; comparing Spiritual things with Spiritual.*
[14] *But the natural man receives not the things of the Spirit of God: for they are foolishness unto him: neither can he know them, because they are Spiritually discerned*   I Corinthians 2: 12-14

The unbeliever has a Spirit, but it is a *carnal spirit* opposed to holy spiritual things and cannot interact with God because the unbeliever does not have the Holy Spirit to guide and teach him. Without the Holy Spirit, the unbeliever has no moral compass and will be completely consumed by things of the world. Only the Soul lives on at physical death. *Where does the soul go when man dies*?

The Answer to this question can be found in both the Old Testament and the New Testament. In general, where the soul of man goes death is seriously misunderstood and poorly taught in the church today. The answer will surprise you.

The Old Testament

The Old Testament has much to say about where the soul goes at physical death. Under the *Old Covenant*, all people regardless of race, color or ethnic background were either a *Jew* or a *Gentile*. The Jews were God's chosen people and the Gentiles were all other people. The Jews lived under the Law which was given to the people by Moses at Mt. Sinai. The Gentiles lived under a law unto themselves.

For when the Gentiles, which have not the law, do by nature the things contained in the law, these, having not the law, are a law unto themselves   Romans 2:14

Regardless of whether a person was a Jew or a Gentile, everyone who ever lived was born a sinner because of Adam's original sin. The Jews were expected to follow the 10 commandments and the other 113 components of the law which were given to them by God. The Law condemned but it was good because God himself established commands called the law, and God is Holy. However, no person could ever live under the law.... It was impossible. The apostle Paul said this about the Law.

[19] *Now we know that what things soever the law saith, it saith to them who are under the law: that every mouth may be stopped, and all the world may become guilty before God.*
[20] *Therefore by the deeds of the law there shall no flesh be justified in his sight: for by the law is the knowledge of sin*   Romans 3: 19-20

...the law was our schoolmaster to bring us unto Christ, that we might be justified Galatians 3:24.

If all who lived under the law were cursed and died in sin, then: *How could anyone be saved?* The answer is that anyone who lived and died under the Law was saved in exactly the same way that Jews and Gentiles are saved today......*By faith*. Every Old Covenant Jew knew that they would die in sin. If they all died in sin then how were they saved? Anyone who might be saved died in the faith of Abraham that God would not abandon them, but He would one day send a Messiah who would forgive their sins and redeem them from the curse of sin.

[15] *Because the law worketh wrath: for where no law is, there is no transgression.*
[16] *Therefore it is of **faith**, that it might be by grace; to the end the promise might*

*be sure to all the seed; not to that only which is of the law, but to that also which is of **the faith of Abraham**; who is the father of us all*   Romans 4: 15-16

The Faith of Abraham was that he would die in sin, but that he would not perish like those who had no faith. King David had this kind of faith.

For thou wilt not leave my soul in hell; neither wilt thou suffer thine Holy One to see corruption   Psalms 16:10

We will shortly see exactly what David was saying in Psalms 16. The following graphic will frame our subsequent discussion.

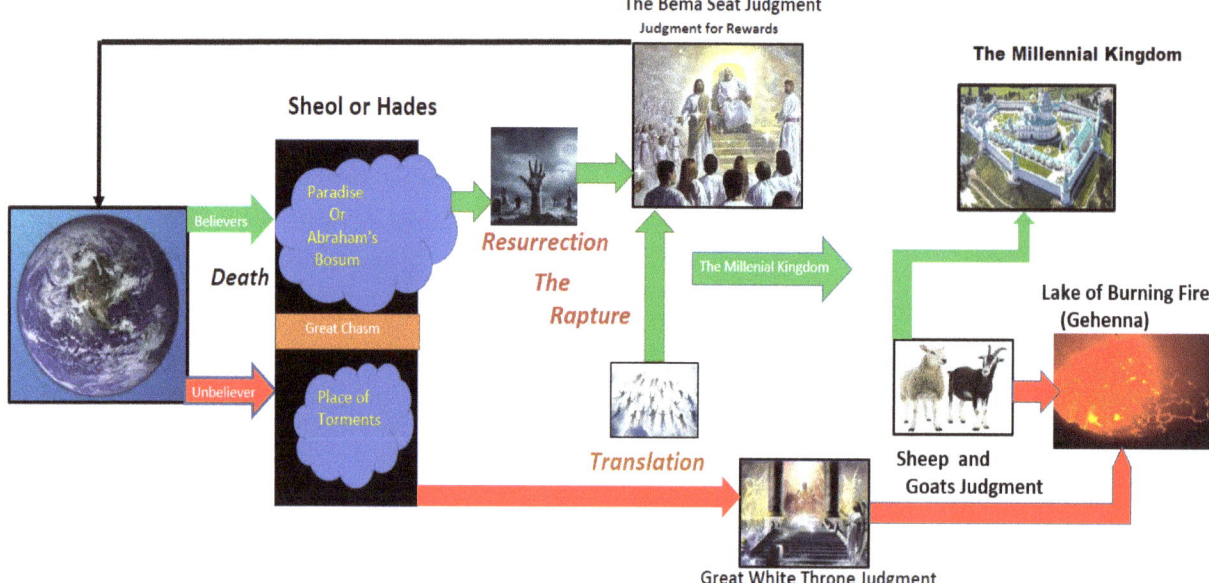

It is taught by the Jewish Rabbis and can be verified from the Old Testament that when a person dies their soul is transported to a place called *Sheol* or *Hades* in the Hebrew language. *Sheol* or *Hades* is composed of two compartments: *Paradise* and a *Place of Torments*. In the Old Testament the word *sheol* was translated from the Hebrew word *She'ole'*. When the Hebrew Old Testament scriptures and the Greek New Testament was translated into Greek, the word *Hell* was used for Sheol. The first mention of hell in the Old Testament is found in Deuteronomy.

*For a fire is kindled in mine anger, and shall burn unto the lowest **hell**, and shall consume the earth with her increase, and set on fire the foundations of the mountains*   Deuteronomy 32:22

The Hebrew word translated as hell in this verse is *She'ole'*. Christ seemed to refer to hell in the New Testament, but it was not She'ole'.

But I say unto you: Whosoever is angry with his brother without a cause shall be in danger of the judgment: and whosoever shall say to his brother, Raca, shall be in danger of the council: but whosoever shall say: Thou fool, shall be in danger of **hell** *fire*   Matthew 5:22

The Greek word translated as *hell* in Matthew 5 is *Gehenna*. Gehenna is *not* hell, but it is a subterranean compartment called the *Lake of Burning Fire* (Revelation 19:20). We will subsequently discuss the Lake of Burning Fire in some detail. For now, understand that the New Testament word for *hell* is used (improperly) to represent many Hebrew or Greek places. Hell is consistently mistranslated in the New Testament from *Gehenna*. The dedicated and informed biblical scholar must recognize that there is no place, anywhere, that is formally named hell. Hell is an invention and mistranslation of the translators.

The authorized King James Version of the Holy Bible uses the word *hell* 64 times throughout the Old and New Testaments. The translated word *hell* does not always come from *Sheole* or *Gehenna*, but also from the word *Tartarus*. Tartarus is another subterranean chamber where 200 fallen angels have been incarcerated since they left heaven to visit earth and engage in sexual intercourse with beautiful women. The offspring were said to be giants known as *Nephilim* (II Peter 2:4). Sheole or *Gehenna* is a place where all unbelievers are sent after they have stood before God at the Great White Throne Judgment. Gehenna is translated as the *Lake of Burning Fire* in Revelation 20:15, and as the *Lake of Fire and Brimstone* in Revelation 19:20 and Revelation 20:10.

[13] *And the sea gave up the dead which were in it; and death and* **hell** *delivered up the dead which were in them: and they were judged every man according to their works.*
[14] *And death and* **hell** *were cast into the lake of fire. This is the second death.*
[15] *And whosoever was not found written in the book of life was cast into the* **lake of fire**   Revelation 20: 13-15

In Revelation 20: 13-15 the Greek word for **hell** is *hades,* which is *Sheole* in Hebrew. Sheole is an area which was composed of Paradise and the Place of Torments. Sheole is found in the Holy Bible 24 times; it is translated as *Hades* 11 times; as *Pit* 3 times; as *hell* 10 times; and as *grave* once. Sheole is *never* translated correctly. Adding to all of this confusion is that two other Greek words are also incorrectly translated as *hell…….* These are *Tartarus* which is used once and *Gehenna* which is used 12 times. Because of the consistently incorrect translation, any place called *hell* in the KJV of the bible is misunderstood to be a place of torment where the souls of the wicked reside. The truth is that there is not one single word in the New or Old Testaments that in its root form means hell. Any word translated as *hell* immediately forms an image of everlasting agony and punishment. Almost every Christian believes that Christ went to such a place after His death, but this is because the Catholic Apostles Creed said in part: *H*e (Christ) *descended into hell*. This is an incorrect usage of hell. Hell is a concept which was a man-invented, pagan and heretical belief, that was first embraced and taught by the early Roman Catholic Church. The term hell was then incorporated into an early translation of the Holy Bible by Jerome, which was a translation of the Holy Bible into Latin, which became known as the *Latin Vulgate*.

In the Old Testament, the soul of a believer and an unbeliever was taken to a place called *Paradise* or *Torments*. The souls of all Old Testament saints before God established the Nation of Israel, and who died believing with the same faith as Abraham, were taken to the place called Paradise to await redemption and final judgment. Psalms 89:48 speaks of death as the instant in which the soul *separates* from the body. This was true before Jesus Christ conquered death and the grave, but *where does the soul of all New Covenant Believers go* after death?

New Testament: Destiny of the Soul

We have shown that Old Testament saints were saved in exactly the same way that Gentiles and Jews are saved today…by *faith*. Old Testament saints knew that they were sinners and could not inherit eternal life under the Law. They believed with the faith of Abraham that God would one day send a redeemer and Messiah who would rescue them from their sins (Job 19:25, Isaiah 14:14, Daniel 9: 25-272. The name and exact time that God would send a Messiah was unknown, but the approximate time of redemption was known from the 70-week prophecy of Daniel (Daniel 9: 27). By 25 AD-26 AD, expectations were running high. In the Fall of 26 AD, John the Baptist was Baptizing Jews unto repentance in the River Jordan. John looked up and when he saw Jesus coming proclaimed: *Behold the Lamb of God who takes away the sins of the world* (John 1:29). Beginning at the River Jordan in 26 AD, Jesus began His ministry of reconciliation to the Jews. In the spring of 30 AD at the *Feast of Pentecost,* he died for the remission of all sin (past, present and future).

During the past 2000 years, Jews and Gentiles have lived and died. Over that period of time, *all* people of faith have died and their souls were taken to *Paradise* to await the blessed hope of Jesus Christ. The souls of all those who died without faith that a Messiah would be sent from God to forgive all sins were transported to a place in Gehenna called *torments*. After the Church Age and the Great Tribulation is over, all *believers* will be judged for rewards, be clothed in robes of white, and receive crowns of glory at the *Bema Seat Judgment*. The souls of all heathens and *unbelievers* are taken to a *Place of Torments*. They will remain there until after the 1000-year *Millennial Kingdom* where they will be judged at the *Great White Throne* Judgment. …. both are two compartments which compose a place called *Sheole*.

When Christ died, he descended into *hell*. This means that He descended into *Sheol*, which is where both *Paradise* and the *Place of Torments* were located. He descended into Paradise and *not* into the Place of Torments. This is proven when He turned to the thief on the cross and told him that after both had died, they would be in Paradise. Before the death of Christ, the Old Covenant was in place…. after Christ died the New Covenant had been initiated.

*And Jesus said unto him, Verily I say unto thee: Today shalt thou be with me in **paradise**.* Luke 23:43

When any person dies today, their soul is also taken to Sheole to either *Paradise* or a *Place of Torments*. The souls of all believers are taken to Paradise, and the souls of all unbelievers are taken to Place of Torments. The souls in Paradise will remain there in a state of happiness and bliss until God calls them forth to be with Him at what we call the *rapture*. The souls which are being held in *Torments* will remain there in a state of torment and anguish until they are called to the *Great White Throne Judgment*.

Mainstream denominational teaching is to overwhelmingly assert that when a Christian dies today, his/her soul is immediately transported to heaven. This theology is intended to make Christians feel good and has no basis in biblical teaching. The main proof-text from which this comes from was spoken by Paul and is found in Philippians.

For I am in a strait betwixt two, having a desire to depart, and to be with Christ; which is far better Philippians 1: 23

Many have assumed from Paul's words to the church at Philippi that he believed that at the moment of his death his consciousness would leave his body to join Christ in heaven. *But is this the case?* Before we analyze what Paul said, it is worth considering what *he did not say*. Paul did not say or even imply that if he died on that day *when* he would be joining Christ. Neither is there any indication of *where* he might be going at the moment he died. To read into Paul's comment the answer to both of these questions is dangerous and cannot be substantiated. Paul is writing from prison in Rome, but he is still witnessing strong for the Lord as evidenced by this letter and previous comments in Philippians 1. He is simply struggling with his current dilemma, and he is not sure if it would be better to stay and fight the good fight or to be with the Lord. If we look further into what Paul wrote to Timothy, it is clear when he expects to join Christ after his earthly ministry is over on that day…... Which is referring to when Christ will return again at the rapture and rescue all of those souls waiting in Paradise.

[6] *For I am now ready to be offered, and the time of my departure is at hand.*
[7] *I have fought a good fight, I have finished my course, I have kept the faith*:
[8] *Henceforth there is laid up for me a crown of righteousness,* **which the Lord, the righteous judge, shall give me at that day**: *and not to me only, but unto* **all them** *also that love* **his appearing**   II Timothy 4: 6-8

Paul is confident that he will be with the Lord, but that this cannot happen until he is judged. He will be judged on *that day* and He will not be alone…. all that wait for the glorious appearing of Jesus Christ will also be there.

This is verified by the story of a rich man and a beggar named Lazarus who died (Luke 16). Some claim that this story was a parable, but parables never use specific names and specific places…. this is a true story.

[19] *There was a certain rich man, which was clothed in purple and fine linen, and fared sumptuously:*
[20] *And there was a certain beggar named Lazarus, which was laid at his gate, full of sores,*
[21] *And desiring to be fed with the crumbs which fell from the rich man's table: moreover the dogs came and licked his sores.*
[22] *And it came to pass, that the beggar died, and was carried by the angels into* **Abraham's bosom**: *the rich man also died, and was buried;*
[23] *And in* **hell** *he lift up his eyes,* **being in torments**, *and saw Abraham afar off, and Lazarus in his bosom.*

[24] And he cried and said, Father Abraham, have mercy on me, and send Lazarus, that he may dip the tip of his finger in water, and cool my tongue; for I am tormented in this flame.
[25] But Abraham said, Son, remember that thou in thy lifetime received thy good things, and likewise Lazarus evil things: but now he is comforted, and thou art tormented.
[26] And beside all this, between us and you there is a great gulf fixed: so that they which would pass from hence to you cannot; neither can they pass to us, that would come from thence   Luke 16: 19-26

The Greek word translated as *hell* is *hades*, which is composed of two separate compartments....one for believers and one for unbelievers. *Abrahams Bosom* is New Testament term for *Paradise*, and *torments* is a New Testament term for *Place of Torments*.

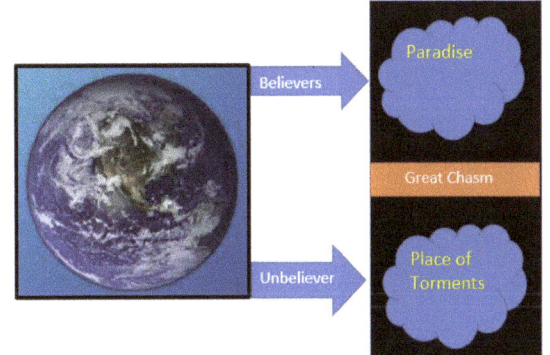

The beggar died and was taken to a place called *Abrahams Bosom* and the rich man died and was taken to a place called *Torments*. One could be seen from another, but between them was a great *chasm* which no one could cross (Luke 17: 19-31).

When Jesus Christ died on the Cross of Calvary, He went to *Paradise* with the repentant thief who was also crucified (Luke 23:43). We know that he *descended* into Paradise (Ephesians 4: 8-9). After the prophesied 3 days and 3 nights that He spent in the tomb had passed, He first appeared before Mary.

*Jesus saith unto her: Touch me not; for I am not yet **ascended** to my Father*
John 20:17

After 3 days and 3 nights, Christ ascended to heaven where He was accepted as the perfect and pure lamb of God who was sacrificed for our sins. This ended both the Levitical priesthood and the sacrifice of bulls and goats as an *atonement* (temporary covering) for sin. Although Christ was the perfect sacrifice for all sin and His death ended temple sacrifices in 30 AD (Phillips, *The Birth of Christ: A Forensic Analysis*), it would be 40 years before God would destroy Herod's temple with the Roman Centurions led by Titus in 70 AD. After receiving His new glorified body, Christ returned to Paradise and evidently moved it to the 3rd heaven.

[4] *There is one body, and one Spirit, even as ye are called in one hope of your calling;*
[5] *One Lord, one faith, one baptism,*
[6] *One God and Father of all, who is above all, and through all, and in you all.*
[7] *But unto every one of us is given grace according to the measure of the gift of Christ.*
[8] ***Wherefore he saith, When he ascended up on high, he led captivity captive, and gave gifts unto men.***
[9] **(Now that he ascended, what is it but that he also descended first into the lower parts of the earth)**?   Ephesians 4: 4-9

Ephesians 4:9 has puzzled biblical scholars for years. After His death on the cross, He *descended* into the lower parts of the earth to Paradise where those Old Testament saints of faith had waited patiently for their redeemer to come…... and now he had arrived to rescue them from Paradise (Ephesians 4: 8-9). The scriptures teach that after 3 days and 3 nights Jesus Christ *ascended* to Heaven. When he ascended into heaven, He evidently moved the subterranean compartment of Paradise up to the 3rd heaven where God dwells. **Ephesians 4:8-9 seems to say** that the occupants of Sheol (Abraham's bosom or Paradise) are taken to heaven…. Christ *descended* into paradise and then *ascended* to Heaven **taking captivity captive**. Not only did Christ take all Old Testament Saints into the 3rd heaven, but He also moved Paradise there as well. The apostle Paul seemed to confirm this conjecture.

[2] *I knew a man in Christ above fourteen years ago, (whether in the body, I cannot tell; or whether out of the body, I cannot tell: God knoweth;) such an one caught up to the third heaven*
[3] *And I knew such a man, (whether in the body, or out of the body, I cannot tell: God knoweth;)*
[4] *How that **he was caught up into paradise**, and heard unspeakable words, which it is not lawful for a man to utter*   II Corinthians 12: 2-4

The truth which is now made manifest to all true believers also solves a puzzling problem which has confounded theologians for years. In Revelation 4: 1-2 the apostle John had just been called to Heaven *in the Spirit* to observe what would take place in the end-times during the Great Tribulation (Revelation 4: 1-20). The first thing that John sees is God upon His throne surrounded by *24 elders* sitting upon *24 seats*. Among the 24 elders He sees Jesus Christ (Revelation 5: 5-6). The 24 elders sing a *new song*:

*And round about the throne were four and twenty seats: and upon the seats I saw four and twenty **elders** sitting, clothed in white raiment; and they had on their heads, crowns of gold*   Revelation 4:4

[9] *And **they sung a new song**, saying, Thou art worthy to take the book, and to open the seals thereof: for thou wast slain, and **hast redeemed us to God by thy blood out of every kindred, and tongue, and people, and nation;***
[10] *And **hast made us unto our God Kings and priests**: and we shall reign on the earth.*
[11] *And I beheld, and I heard the voice of many angels round about the throne and the beasts and the elders: and the number of them was ten thousand times ten thousand, and thousands of thousands*   Revelation 5: 9-11

This is a very perplexing passage of scripture. John has just arrived in heaven and this is the first thing he sees. Note carefully that: (1) They are all clothed in white (2) They wear Crowns of Gold ......Revelation 4:4 (3) They hold harps and vials of prayers from Saints .... Revelation 5:8 (3) They sing a *new song......Revelation 5:9* (4) They will reign upon the earth.... Revelation 5:10). These seem to be saints who have assumed places of service to God, and not angels. This conjecture is reinforced and made almost certain by Revelation 5:9.

 And they sung a new song, saying: Thou (Jesus Christ) *art worthy to take the book, and to open the seals thereof: for thou wast slain, and **hast redeemed us to God by thy blood out of every kindred, and tongue, and people, and nation***
Revelation 5:9

These are clearly identified as redeemed saints from every race, creed and color..... not created heavenly beings (angels). *If this is true, then where did they come from?* The only place that they could have come from is from the Old Testament believers who had patiently waited in the heart of the earth for Jesus Christ to arrive in Paradise, and as previously conjectured they were moved *up* to the 3rd heaven after 3 days and 3 nights. This is consistent with the position that the Jews have always held in the eyes of God. The Jews were chosen by God to be *His* people (Deuteronomy 7:6). The Jews were the *apple of His eye* (Zachariah 2:8) and He took them as His eternal bride (Jeremiah 7:34). The Jews are destined to inherit the promised land, not the saved Gentiles (Genesis 12:7, Genesis 13:15, Genesis 15:18, Genesis 17:8). It is consistent with God's love for His chosen people that he would set them aside for service to Him. This is conjecture by the author, and cannot be proved or disproved by scripture.

There is one more piece of this puzzle which must be put into place. The apostle Paul was chosen by Jesus Christ to reveal the *mystery* of the Church Age and the Body of Christ. In his epistle to the church in Corinth Paul wrote the following.

[2] *I knew a man in Christ above fourteen years ago, (whether in the body, I cannot tell; or whether out of the body, I cannot tell: God knoweth;) such an one caught up to the third heaven*
[3] *And I knew such a man, (whether in the body, or out of the body, I cannot tell: God knoweth;)*
[4] *How that **he was caught up into paradise**, and heard unspeakable words, which it is not lawful for a man to utter*   II Corinthians 12: 2-4

Paul was always trying to glorify God and not himself. He continuously avoided taking the credit for anything. In II Corinthians 12: 2-4 he wrote that he *knew a man* who was **caught up** *into Paradise*. This was undoubtedly Paul himself, but that is not important. What is important is that that a man was **caught up**. When Christ went to Paradise after He was resurrected, he *descended* into Paradise. Evidently, after Jesus left Paradise and was glorified, he moved Paradise from somewhere in the depths of the earth to somewhere in the 3rd heaven. Note that He did not move the Place of Torments where all nonbelievers are now incarcerated. We do know that when Christ ascended to heaven: *He led captivity captive* (Ephesians 4:8). It is proposed that sometime soon after Jesus Christ ascended to heaven, He emptied paradise and presented those that had been held captive there to His Father. This is exactly what would be expected, since those Jews being held in Paradise were the *apple of his eye*, and *His chosen people*. This could explain where the 24 elders and the multitude of people that John saw in heaven came from.

Summary

We have shown from the scriptures that when a righteous man with the Faith of Abraham (Romans 4:3) died in the Old Testament he was taken to *Sheole* to a compartment called *Paradise*. The *souls* of those who had faith that God would send a Messiah who would redeem them and save them from their sins waited patiently for their promised redeemer to free them from Paradise.

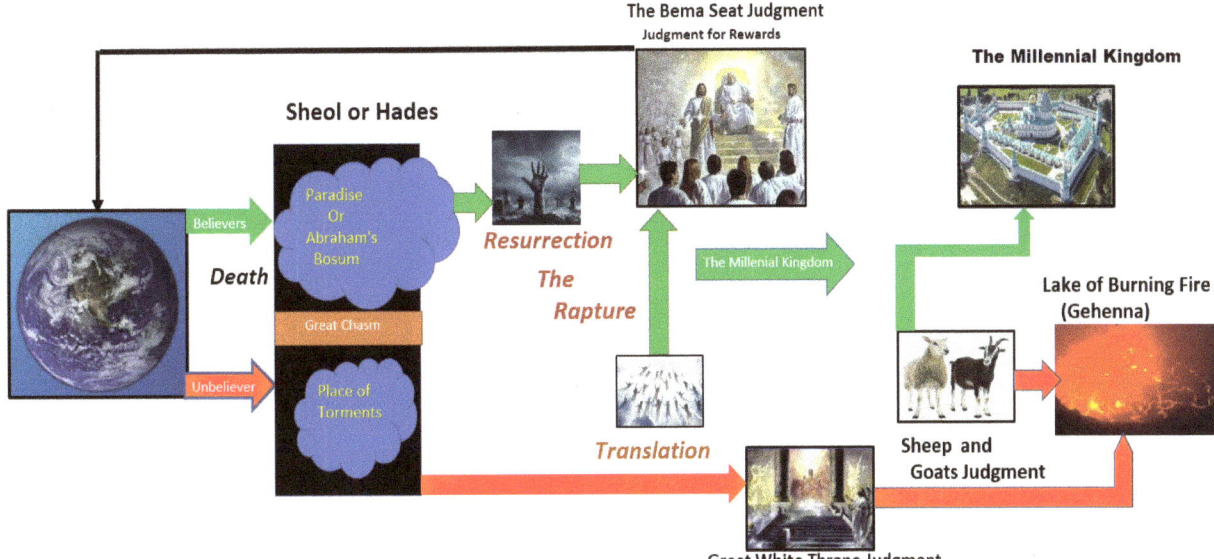

The souls of all unbelievers were taken to a *Place of Torments* where they would be incarcerated until their fate is sealed at the *Great White Throne Judgment*. This will be *after* the 1000-year Millennial Kingdom and *before* the earth is cleansed and eternity begins. When Christ died, He went to Paradise for 3 days and 3 nights during which He presented Himself as their long-awaited Messiah. After He was resurrected by the *power of God* and was glorified, He returned to Paradise. He led *captives in His train* to the Father……and reunited God with His *Bride*…The Jews (Jeremiah 16:9). He then moved Paradise from beneath the earth to the 3rd heaven somewhere near God and His Throne. Jesus Christ will not claim His bride…...the Church…. until He returns again to rapture them to Himself (I Thessalonians 4:17).

During the current Church Age, the souls of all who are born again, accepted Jesus Christ as their Lord and Savior and then died are taken *up* to Paradise where they await the *rapture* of all Saints…living and dead. When Jesus Christ returns to rapture away all true believers, the souls in paradise will at that time supernaturally be united with a renovated, Holy and perfect body from the Grave. They will then be caught up to heaven where they will be judged for rewards at the *Bema Seat Judgment*.

This judgment will occur *after* the Church Age has ended and *before* the 10000-year Millennial Kingdom begins. What about the *unbelievers* incarcerated in the *Place of Torments*? They will be judged not for rewards but for punishment in the *Lake of Burning Fire* at the *Great White Throne Judgment*. All whose names are not written in the *Book of Life* will be cast into the Lake of Burning Fire (Revelation 20: 11-15).

There remains only one judgment which should be described, and that is the *Judgment of the Sheep and Goats* which Jesus Christ will preside over at the end of the Church Age.

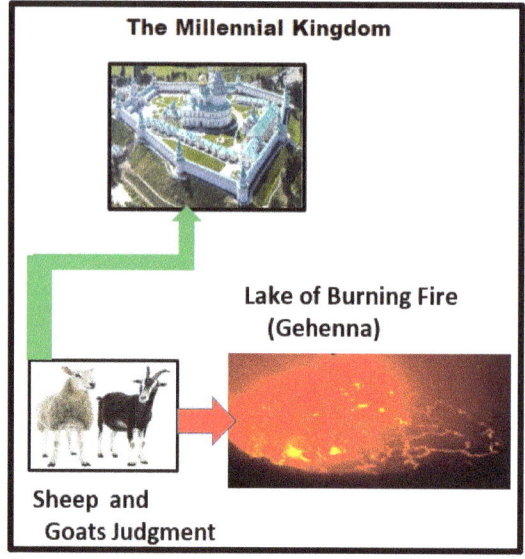

The Great Tribulation will be centered around the Holy City of Jerusalem, and will mostly involve the European Theatre. After the Battle of Armageddon has been fought and won by Jesus Christ, there will be a great multitude of people that were not raptured earlier living in foreign countries and in places throughout the world. Jesus Christ will send His angels to harvest all remaining people from the nations (Matthew 25: 31-32). The Church Age has just ended and so has salvation by faith and grace. Hence, Jesus will *judge people from all nations* (Matthew 25: 31-32) based upon how they treated both *His people* and the *poor and strangers* (Matthew 25: 34-45). Those who had protected and nourished those people would be called *sheep*....and He will send them to His *right*. Those who persecuted and tormented those people would be called *goats*......and he will send them to His *left* 9Matthew 25:33). The Goats will be condemned to everlasting punishment and the sheep into life eternal. This proves by the very words of Jesus Christ that the soul will live forever, and that that a soul will live in everlasting punishment or in joy and happiness. Note that this is after the Age of Grace or the Church Age has ended.

In conclusion: *Does the soul of a New Covenant Christian immediately go to heaven when that person dies?* NO.

All scripture is given by inspiration of God, and is profitable for doctrine, for reproof, for correction, for instruction in righteousness
II Timothy 3:16

Study to shew thyself approved unto God, a workman that need not to be ashamed, rightly dividing the word of truth.   II Timothy 2:15

You will know the truth, and the truth will set you free   John 8:32

But Jesus answered them: "You are wrong, because you know neither the Scriptures nor the power of God"   Matthew 22: 29

Think over what I say, for the Lord will give you understanding in everything.   II Timothy 2:7

I shall be telling this with a sigh
Somewhere ages and ages hence:
Two roads diverged in a wood, and I....
I took the one less traveled by,
And that has made all the difference.

Chapter 7

The Seven Feasts of Israel

It is impossible to correctly understand the sequence of end-time events without understanding the historical and prophetic meanings of the *Seven Feasts of Israel*. They provide a blueprint for both the 1st and the 2nd comings of Jesus Christ. The Seven Feasts of Israel were ordained by God shortly after the law was given at Mt. Sinai following the exodus from Egypt. They were given for two reasons. The *first* was to commemorate the deliverance of Israel from Egyptian bondage and oppression. The *second* was to prophesy of Seven events which will herald the first and second coming of Jesus Christ. The first four Feasts are held in the spring, and the last three in the fall. The first four Feasts were fulfilled at the death and resurrection of Jesus Christ. The last three will be fulfilled as the 70th week of Daniel and when this current age comes to a close.

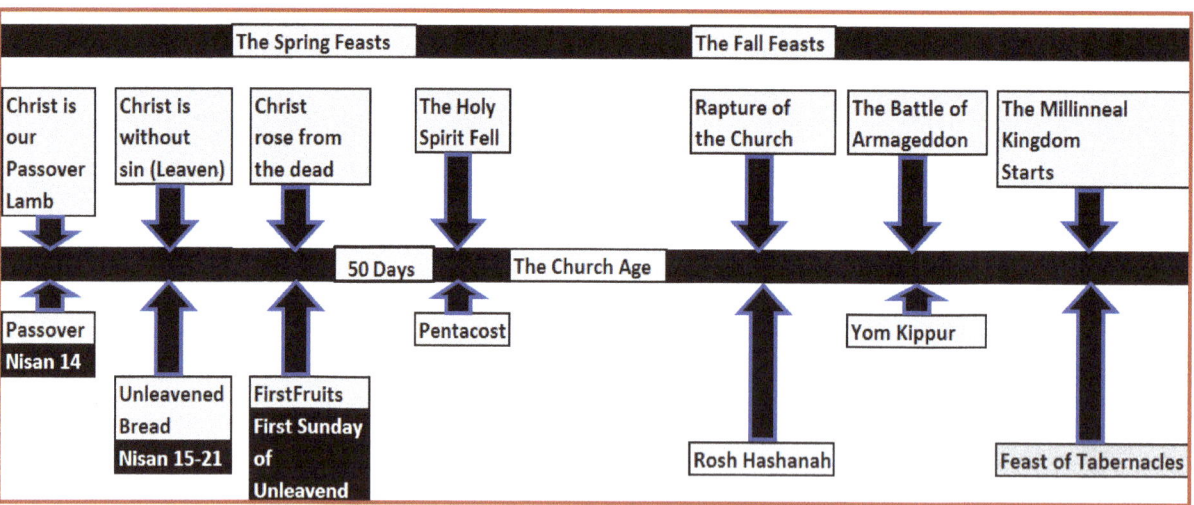

The Seven Feasts and their appointed time on the ancient Hebrew calendar are shown in the following table.

	Feast	Hebrew Date
1	Passover (Pesah)	Nisan 14
2	Unleavened Bread	Nisan 15-21
3	FirstFruits	Lasts 50 days, starting on 1st Sunday of Unleavened Bread
4	Pentecost (Weeks)	50th day of Feast of Weeks
5	Trumpets (Rosh Hashanna)	Tishri 1
6	Yom Kippur (Atonement)	Tishri 10
7	Tabernacles (Booths)	Tishri 15-22

The original Hebrew calendar was a *lunar* calendar. It was composed of 12 months alternating between 29 and 30 days per month. Each month started on the new moon. From new moon to new moon is approximately 29.5306 days. Since days must be whole numbers, it is obvious why they alternated between 29 and 30 days in length. Note that a 12-month year was 354 days long. This created a problem because a year is determined not by the moon, but by the sun, and a solar year is about 365 days in length (365.2422 days). Without some sort of adjustment, the Hebrew 354-day, 12-month year would *fall behind* a solar year at a rate of about 10.872 days every year. In other words, if unadjusted about every 17 years a fall festival would occur in the spring! It was determined long ago that to keep the two calendars (lunar and solar) in sync with one another, a 13th month of 29/30 days, called Adar II, was inserted Seven times over a 19-year cycle. This proved to be very accurate, but because Adar II was inserted only periodically, the date of each of the Seven Feasts wandered through about two months. For example, Tishri 1 would some years start in September and some in October. Modern Jewish calendars use other sophisticated rules to regulate the yearly calendar and keep it in sync with a solar year, but each feast still *wanders* across two months. Modern computers have been programmed to accurately calculate the month, day and day of the week back through thousands of years. We will not elaborate further on the operation of the Jewish calendar, but it is a fascinating and rewarding study. We will now concentrate on what each festival means, both historically and prophetically, and refer to when each festival occurs by its Jewish name and Jewish calendar date. There is, however, one important historical event which we must explore: God's renumbering of the Hebrew calendar months at the exodus from Egypt. The Hebrew calendar has existed from earliest time. The ancient book of *Jubilees* records that Enoch *understood* the movement of the sun, moon and stars and was told by angels how calendars operate. In the flood account recorded in Genesis, it is clear that a calendar was in use. Moving forward in time, when the Children of Israel were in Egypt before the Exodus, there was a very good Egyptian calendar. It consisted of 12 months of 30 days, and at the end of every year five extra days were added. This made an Egyptian year 365 days long, so it only dropped back from the solar year about one day every four years. Even this made a large difference eventually. Both before and after the Exodus, we have no definitive biblical records of what calendar was used by the Hebrews. However, after the exodus from Egypt, the Feast of Firstfruits had to occur just as the barley crop was maturing in the field, because the high priest had to *wave a firstfruit* offering of barley to the Lord before anything could be harvested. It is clear that the month of Nisan was somehow started every year based upon how the crop was maturing, possibly by observing the crop of barley as it matured and inserting an extra month if the crop was not going to be ready for a *Firstfruits harvest* on Nisan

15. Winding forward about 1000 years the nation of Israel fell to the Babylonian Empire. Virtually the whole nation was deported to Babylon for a period of 70 years for failing to observe Sabbatical and Jubilee years. The Babylonians had a deep knowledge of how calendars operated, and the Hebrews adopted both the Babylonian calendrical system and the names of each month with minor variations. We have biblical and historical records that confirm a sophisticated calendar was in effect and was being maintained by the Levitical priesthood soon after the Babylonian exile of 70 years had been completed.

As previously stated, the *Seven Feasts of Israel* are divided into two separate seasons of the year. The Feasts of Passover, Firstfruits, Unleavened Bread and Pentecost all take place in the spring. The last three Feasts of Rosh Hashanah, Yom Kippur, and Tabernacles take place in the fall. The Feasts have a dual meaning; they commemorate the deliverance of the Hebrew nation from Egyptian bondage, and they also prophesy of the first and second coming of Jesus Christ. The Hebrew word for feast is *moed* which means a *set time* or an *appointed time*. God has not only set an appointed time for each feast, he has also commanded that every male in Israel must be at the place of his choice (Jerusalem) for the Feasts of Passover, Unleavened Bread, Pentecost and Tabernacles. The Feasts are also called a *holy convocation*. The Hebrew word for convocation means *rehearsal*. The implication is that God has commanded the Children of Israel to observe each feast at the *appointed time* as *a rehearsal* for seven things which will happen to Israel on those days. LooKing back, it is now obvious that Jesus Christ fulfilled the first four Feasts at His crucifixion between when He died on the cross of Calvary and when He sent the Holy Spirit to dwell in man on the Feast of Passover. The last three Feasts will be fulfilled at the second advent of Christ. All Seven Feasts were divinely ordained by God and given to the nation of Israel for a perpetual observance.

The historical and physical aspects of each feast will now be briefly discussed.

The Spring Feasts

Feast of Passover (Nisan 14)

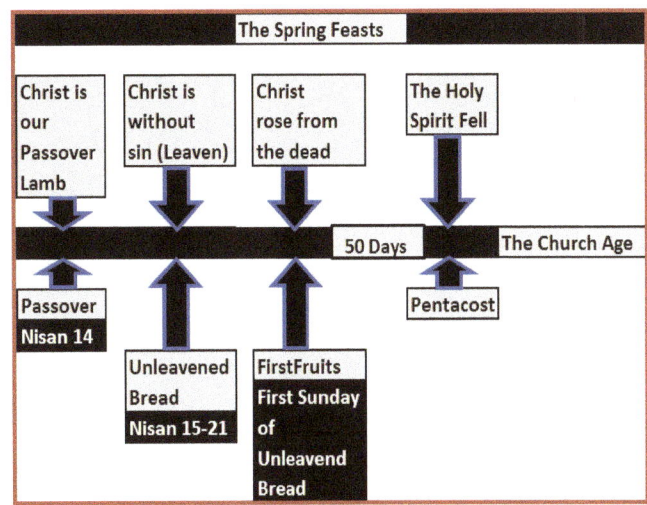

The Feast of Passover is in remembrance of the night that the Hebrew nation left Egypt on Nisan 15 (Exodus 12:2-11). On Nisan 10, God instructed the Children of Israel to select an unblemished lamb one year old and bring it into each house for four days. Each day the lamb was examined to make sure that it was still unblemished. On *Nisan 14* at 3:00 pm, they were instructed to slaughter the lamb and prepare it for the evening meal. The blood was to be caught in a bowl, and smeared over the lintel or over the door of each Hebrew house. The lamb was to be eaten that evening, which was actually the first few hours of Nisan 15. At midnight, the *Avenging Angel* of the Lord would pass over every house in Egypt. The firstborn male in any house without blood over the door would be killed, and the firstborn of all livestock outside the house would be killed (Gen 12:29). This was the event that caused the Pharaoh of Egypt to *let the people go* after his firstborn son was slain. The Feast of Passover was to commemorate and recall remembrance of this event for perpetual generations.

Spiritual Application: Jesus Christ arrived in Jerusalem on Nisan 10 (after 6:00pm) and stayed at the house of Lazarus exactly four days before He was to be crucified on Nisan 14. He was examined and scrutinized by the Sadducees and Pharisees who sought to discredit Him. He was found to be without spot or blemish. Pilate even declared: **Then said Pilate to the chief priests and to the people, I find no fault in this man** (Luke 23:4). Christ completely fulfilled the Feast of Passover when He was crucified on the cross of Calvary.

For even Christ our Passover is sacrificed for us　　　　I Corinthians 5:7

The next day John sees Jesus coming unto him, and said: Behold the Lamb of God, which taketh away the sin of the world　　　　John 1:29

The word *Passover* is literally translated *Lamb* and Christ is God's perfect Passover sacrificial lamb. He was both the sacrifice and the one who offered the sacrifice.

For even Christ our Passover is sacrificed for us   I Corinthians 5:7

Our Lord Jesus Christ died for our sins at 3:00 pm on Nisan 14, at exactly the same time that the High Priest was killing the Passover Lamb in the temple. At that time the veil that separated the Holy Place from the Holy of Holies was *rent in two* from top to bottom, signifying that the Levitical sacrificial system had ended. The old covenant had passed away; the new covenant had now come.

Feast of Unleavened Bread (Nisan 15-21)
The Feast of Unleavened Bread is a memorial to when the Children of Israel left Egypt in haste on the evening of Nisan 14, which was the night portion of Nisan 15. The Feast of Unleavened Bread started at 6:00 pm on Wednesday and continued for seven full days until 6:00 pm on Nisan 21. It is important to note that both Nisan 15 and Nisan 21 were designated as a *High Sabbath*. On these days there was to be no unleavened bread in any household. No servile work was to be done on these days, and if food is to be consumed it must be prepared by the family in their house. The Exodus from Egypt was sudden. In Exodus 12 we are told: *So the people took their dough before it was leavened, having their kneading bowls bound and in their clothes on their shoulders* (Exodus 12:34). When the Feast of Unleavened Bread was observed in subsequent years, starting with Nisan 15 there was to be no leavened bread at all in any household for Seven days. All leaven was to be removed on Nisan 14. This was serious business.

For Seven days no leaven shall be found in your houses, since whoever eats what is leavened, that same person shall be cut off from the congregation of Israel, whether he is a stranger or a native of the land   Exodus 12:19

In Exodus 16:2, the Israelites complained that they had no food, so God miraculously provided *manna* to them every day. The manna was picked in the morning on Sunday-Friday. It only lasted one day; the manna picked on Friday morning lasted two days and then spoiled on the third day to honor the Jewish Sabbath (Saturday). Moses put a *pot of manna* into the Ark of the Covenant; it *never* spoiled.

Spiritual Application: In the scriptures, *leaven* is representative of *sin*. Our Lord Jesus Christ fulfilled all of the law. His life was perfect in every way. He was the unleavened, sinless bread from heaven. Since He was sinless, He was without *spot or blemish*. He was resurrected and lifted up to God, and He was an acceptable and perfect sacrifice to God.

Your glorying is not good. Know ye not that a little leaven leavens the whole lump? Purge out therefore the old leaven, that ye may be a new lump, as ye are unleavened. For even Christ our Passover is sacrificed for us   I Corinthians 5:6-7

Our Lord Jesus Christ said that He was the Unleavened Bread which fulfilled the feast.

And as they did eat, Jesus took bread, and blessed, and broke it, and gave to them, and said, Take, eat: this is my body   Mark 14:22

And Jesus said unto them, I am the bread of life: he that cometh to me shall never hunger; and he that believeth on me shall never thirst   John 6:35

I am the bread of life. He who comes to me shall never hunger   John 6:35

He was also the *manna that never spoiled*, eternally perfect.

I am the living bread which came down from heaven: if any man eat of this bread, he shall live forever: and the bread that I will give is my flesh, which I will give for the life of the world. This is that bread which came down from heaven: not as your fathers did eat manna, and are dead: he that eats of this bread shall live forever John 6:51, 58

Christ was crucified on Nisan 14. He *gave up the ghost* and died at 3:00 pm, at exactly the same time that the High Priest in Herod's Temple slaughtered the Passover lamb. Jesus was placed in the tomb just in time to fulfill the *Feast of Unleavened Bread* which started at 6:00 pm on Wednesday night. Jesus was our perfect Passover Lamb, without spot or blemish. He was also the perfect *Bread of Life*, without leaven (sin).

Feast of Firstfruits
The Feast of Firstfruits is *also* called the *Feast of Weeks*. Both unlike the Feast of Passover and the Feast of Unleavened Bread, it has a specific day of the week (Sunday) when it is observed, but not a specific day of the Jewish month.

Speak unto the Children of Israel, and say unto them: When ye be come into the land which I give unto you, and shall reap the harvest thereof, then ye shall bring a sheaf of the firstfruits of your harvest unto the priest: And he shall wave the sheaf before the LORD, to be accepted for you: on the morrow after the Sabbath the priest shall wave it. And ye shall offer that day when ye wave the sheaf and the lamb without blemish of the first year for a burnt offering unto the LORD. And the meat offering thereof shall be two tenth deals of fine flour mingled with oil, an offering made by fire unto the LORD for a sweet savor: and the drink offering thereof shall be of wine, the fourth part of a hin. And ye shall eat neither bread, nor parched corn, nor green ears, until the selfsame day that ye have brought an offering unto your God: it shall be a statute forever throughout your generations in all your dwellings. And ye shall count unto you from the morrow after the sabbath, from the day that ye brought the sheaf of the wave offering; Seven sabbaths shall be complete: Even unto the morrow after the seventh sabbath shall ye number fifty days; and ye shall offer a new meat offering unto the Lord   Leviticus 23:10-16

The Feast of Firstfruits starts on the *morrow after the Sabbath*. There was a raging battle between the Pharisees and the Sadducees as to what this means. The first day of the Feast of Unleavened Bread was a *Sabbath*, a *High Sabbath*. The Pharisees held that the Feast of Firstfruits started on Nisan 16 every year, while the Sadducees maintained that it started on the day after the *weekly Sabbath* (Saturday). The above passage says that *Seven Sabbaths must be complete* in the 50-day period. This is Seven complete weeks, and is referred to as the *Feast of Weeks*. The term feast of Weeks is not quite correct. It is not a feast at all, but actually refers to the 7 complete Sabbath cycles (49 days) that take place between the *Feast of Firstfruits* and the *Feast of Pentecost*. This will happen every year if the feast starts on the Sunday following the only Sabbath (Saturday) of Unleavened Bread. Eventually the Sadducees prevailed but the controversy remained. The real key is in the spiritual fulfillment of this feast by Jesus Christ. Christ rose early on a Sunday, and he is the *firstfruits* of the church, so the feast must also begin on a Sunday to satisfy typology. It actually takes place on Sunday morning in the temple. In the time of Jesus, the Feasts of Passover, Unleavened Bread and Firstfruits were considered to be one long feast season which was generally referred to as the *Passover Season*. It was not uncommon to refer to all three as simply *Passover*. The Feast of Firstfruits signified the early maturation of the *barley* crop and the beginning of a long growing season for *wheat*. The Feast of Firstfruits was ritually observed by all Jews throughout the temple eras. The *Firstfruit Offerings* were to both please God and to support the Levitical priesthood (Leviticus 23:10-17, Exodus 23:19, Deuteronomy 26:1-11). On the first day of the feast, a *sheaf of barley*, which was an *omer* (about 2 quarts), was to be picked from the fields and offered up to God as a wave offering by the High Priest. It was *waved before the Lord* in a sheaf.

Spiritual Application: The firstfruits sheaf was also symbolic of the greater *wheat harvest* to come. If the firstfruit was holy, then the entire harvest would be holy unto the Lord. Paul confirmed the spiritual intent of the firstfruit offering, and directly related it to the *root* (Israel) and the *branches* (the body of Christ).

For if the firstfruit be holy, the lump is also holy: and if the root be holy, so are the branches   Romans 11:16

The firstfruit offering consecrated the entire harvest to the Lord. It was an *earnest offering* or a *pledge* of the full harvest which was yet to come. It was very important, because no barley from the field could be picked or eaten until the ceremony was completed. In fact, ancient tradition held that on Nisan 1 the High Priest would inspect the *barley in the ear*. The word Nisan actually means *green ear*. If the crop had not matured enough by Nisan 1 to pick a *wave sheaf* on Nisan 15, then an extra month of 29/30 days called *Adar II* would be immediately added to the year. While not exact, this was elegant in its simplicity. Periodic insertion of an extra month kept the Jewish lunar-based calendar from getting very far *out of sync* with the solar calendar and the agricultural seasons. It is not known when the *Metonic cycle* was discovered, and exact insertion rules were put into place, but a sophisticated system appeared to be in operation shortly after the Babylonian exile had ended.

The first of the firstfruits of thy land thou shalt bring unto the house of the LORD thy God   Exodus 34:26

How beautiful and prophetic was the firstfruit offering! Christ is everywhere present in the typology. The offering was to be made of *green ears* of corn that would be dried in the fire. Was not our Lord Jesus Christ *tried as if in the fire* by the Pharisees and Sadducees? Was He not tempted at every turn just as we are today? After being offered to the Lord, the dried corn was then to be *beaten* out of the ear for food for the Levites. Was not our Lord Jesus Christ *beaten and bruised* for our sins, and then accepted by God as the firstfruit offering? *Oil* was also to be poured over the firstfruits offering; did Jesus not pour out the *oil* of the Holy Spirit on the day of Pentecost? Today the Feast of Firstfruits is observed by Christians for one day only and is called *Easter*. It is appropriate that Christians observe the resurrection of our risen Savior, but the modern observance called *Easter* has been corrupted. The modern observance of Easter was initiated by the Roman Catholic Church, and received its name from the Babylonian goddess, *Ishtar*. Ishtar is the pagan god of fertility, love, and sex; and that is why eggs are a part of the modern Easter celebration. The same thing is true as to why rabbits are part of the pageantry. Although children use rabbits, colored eggs and green grass to celebrate Easter, adult Christians observe Easter as the day of our Lord's resurrection from the dead. Instead of calling this celebration *Easter*, we should call it *Firstfruits*. There are exactly 50 days (7 full week is also called the *Feast of Weeks*, since it lasts exactly Seven weeks (49 days) and one day. The 50th and final day is called *Shavuot* by the Jews. In 1491 BC the Children of Israel left Egypt during the night of Nisan 15 (Wednesday evening; Thursday on the Jewish calendar). Three days later they crossed the *Sea of Reeds*. They emerged on the other side a free nation, miraculously saved from the armies of the Pharaoh when God drowned all of the pursuers in the Red Sea. Fifty days later, they were given the law by God at Mt. Sinai. On the first day of the Feast of Firstfruits a remarkable thing happened. On that day, our Lord Jesus Christ rose from the grave. Christ arose just as Sunday was *dawning* or about to start just after 6:00 pm. There is no proof in the scriptures that Christ rose from the grave just before daylight on Sunday morning. This is another story that the Catholic Church instituted. To be clear, there is no problem in celebrating Christ's resurrection at a *sunrise service* on Sunday morning, it is holy that we should do so. The point is just that Christ rose early that previous evening just as Sunday began Nisan 17, and not just before sunrise.

But now is Christ risen from the dead, and become the firstfruits of them that slept I Corinthians 15:20

Christ was the *First of the Firstfruits*. He was not the only person that had been resurrected from the dead; but he was the first to ascend to heaven, receive His glorified body, and not taste death again.

For if the firstfruit be holy, the lump is also holy: and if the root be holy, so are the branches Romans 11:16

Christ is the vine and we are the branches. Christ spoke of this during his earthly ministry.

And Jesus answered them, saying: The hour is come, that the Son of man should be glorified. Verily, verily, I say unto you, except a corn of wheat fall into the ground and die, it abides alone: but if it dies, it bringeth forth much fruit. He that loveth his life shall lose it; and he that hates his life in this world shall keep it unto life eternal. If any man serves me, let him follow me; and where I am, there shall also my servant be: if any man serves me, him will my Father honor John 12:23-26

The Apostle Paul made an astonishing statement in his first letter to Corinth.

But now is Christ risen from the dead, and become the firstfruits of them that slept. For since by man came death, by man came also the resurrection of the dead. For as in Adam all die, even so in Christ shall all be made alive. But every man in his own order: Christ the firstfruits; afterward they that are Christ's at his coming. Then cometh the end, when he shall have delivered up the Kingdom to God, even the Father; when he shall have put down all rule and all authority and power
I Corinthians 15:20-24

Christ is clearly called the *firstfruits* of all that *slept* (died). He then goes on to say that following Christ there will one day be a resurrection of the dead. After that, the end (of the age) will come and all *powers, authorities and rulers* will be put under His feet. There is no indication whatsoever that there will be a seven-year period of time between when the resurrection of the dead will occur and the *end*.

Pentecost
The last day of the Feast of Firstfruits and the end of the Feast of Weeks is called *Shavuot*, which we call *Pentecost*. Jewish tradition teaches that on the day of Pentecost the law was given to Israel on Mt. Sinai. There were 50 days that elapsed between when the Children of Israel left Egypt and the law was given at Mt. Sinai. The word *Pentecost* is derived from the Greek word *Penta*, which means fifty. Israel departed Egypt on Nisan 15, and emerged from the Sea of Reeds three days later. This is exactly the same day that Jesus Christ emerged from the grave. In typology, a Friday crucifixion declared by the Roman Catholic Church and the subsequent resurrection from the grave on Sunday is impossible. The Israelites had to move quickly and take a full three days between when they left Egypt and when they arrived at the Red Sea. There is simply no getting around a *full* three-day journey. In order to satisfy type, Christ was in the grave for a *full* three days and three nights. The Children of Israel then traveled 47 days until they finally reached Mt. Sinai. The Lord told the people to sanctify themselves for two days (Gen 19:10), and on the *third* day He would come down to them in a cloud. On the *50th day* after emerging from the Red Sea the Lord kept his promise and appeared to the people. A *Shofar* (trumpet made of a ram's horn) was loudly sounded: louder, and louder, and louder until *fire* was seen on the mountain. A mighty wind blew and the ground shook as if an earthquake was going to occur. At that point God began to deliver the law to Moses and the nation of Israel. It is taught that every nation and every tongue heard the Lord in their own language. According to tradition, there was the Hebrew language and 69 other languages spoken throughout the world. In a miraculous and divine act, the voice

of God was divided into *70 different tongues*. It is also taught by the Rabbis that as God spoke, the Children of Israel not only heard the words but actually saw each word emerging from the cloud as *tongues of fire*. The words encircled the camp and then entered each person individually. After each commandment was given, God asked: ***Do you accept upon yourself this commandment?*** and everyone present answered *yes*. The tongues of fire then fell upon stone tablets and the words of the law were recorded. The Jewish Feast of Shavuot on the 50th day commemorates these events (Joseph Good)

Spiritual Application: When Christ ascended from the grave he commanded his disciples to *go unto Jerusalem* and wait for Him to come to them.

And when the day of Pentecost was fully come, they were all with one accord in one place. And suddenly there came a sound from heaven as of a rushing mighty wind, and it filled all the house where they were sitting. And there appeared unto them cloven tongues like as of fire, and it sat upon each of them. And they were all filled with the Holy Ghost, and began to speak with other tongues, as the Spirit gave them utterance. And there were dwelling at Jerusalem Jews, devout men, out of every nation under heaven. Now when this was noised abroad, the multitude came together, and were confounded, because that every man heard them speak in his own language   Acts 2:1-6

What an amazing event!! On the very day that God gave the law to the people on Mt. Sinai, Jesus Christ gave the Holy Spirit to his chosen people. The falling of the Holy Spirit at Pentecost in 30 AD almost exactly paralleled the giving of the law 1500 years earlier. The law was written on tablets of stone. The *old covenant* was based upon man fulfilling the law, which was impossible. The *new covenant* was based upon grace, and written on the heart of man. The impossible task of living a perfect life under the law was fulfilled in every way by our Lord Jesus Christ, who then imputed His righteousness to all who believed in His name. Only Jesus Christ fulfilled every *jot and tidle* of the law. He was our *perfect Passover sacrifice for sin*, the Lamb of God. He was the *Firstfruits* offering waved before the Lord by Christ himself. He was both the *offerer* and the *offering*, our eternal High Priest. The old covenant that God had established with His people required obedience to the Old Testament Mosaic law. Because the *wages of sin are death* (Romans 6:23), the law required that people perform rituals and sacrifices in order to please God and temporarily cover their sins. The prophet Jeremiah predicted that there would be a time when God would make a new covenant with the nation of Israel.

The day will come said the Lord, when I will make a new covenant with the people of Israel and Judah... But this is the new covenant I will make with the people of Israel on that day, says the Lord. I will put my law in their minds, and I will write them on their hearts. I will be their God, and they will be my people Jeremiah 31:31, 33.

Jesus Christ came to fulfill all of the Law of Moses (Matthew 5:17) and create a new covenant between God and His people. He is now our High Priest who sits on the throne of God and continually intercedes for us.

This is the covenant that I will make with them after those days, saith the Lord, I will put my laws into their hearts, and in their minds will I write them
Hebrews 10:16

The old covenant was written in stone, but the new covenant is written on our hearts, made possible only by faith in Christ who shed His own blood to atone for the sins of the world.

And he took bread, and gave thanks, and broke it, and gave unto them, saying: This is my body which is given for you: this do in remembrance of me. Likewise, also the cup after supper, saying, this cup is the New Testament in my blood, which is shed for you Luke 22:19-20

Now that we are under the new covenant, we are not under the penalty of the law. We are now given the opportunity to receive salvation as a free gift (Ephesians 2:8-9). Through the life-giving Holy Spirit who lives in all believers (Romans 8:9-11), we can now share in the inheritance of Christ.

For this reason, Christ is the mediator of a new covenant, that those who are called may receive the promised eternal inheritance—now that He has died as a ransom to set them free from the sins committed under the first covenant
Hebrews 9:15

Summary of the First Four (Spring) Feasts of Israel
The spring Feasts of Israel are (1) Passover, (2) Unleavened Bread, (3) First Fruits and (4) Pentecost. Each of these Feasts was to provide historical and prophetic truth to the Children of Israel. Christ fulfilled each of these first four Feasts at the end of his 3.5-year earthly ministry. **Passover**: Christ was the perfect Passover Lamb, slain from the foundation of the world. **Unleavened Bread**: Christ was without sin (leaven). He fulfilled the laws given to Moses by God in every way. He is our *bread of life*, and whosoever will eat of His bread will never hunger.

Firstfruits: Christ was the perfect firstfruits offering waved before the Lord and fully accepted. He was the *first* to be raised from the grave never to die again.
Pentecost: Christ ratified the *new covenant* on the Feast of Pentecost 50 days after he arose from the grave, He offered the Holy Spirit as our comforter and guarantee. Salvation is now offered free to all who believe that Jesus Christ is the only Son of God. The curse of the law has been replaced by amazing grace. We who are now called *Christians* can live life *more abundantly*. Every feast was a *moed*, a *set time* or an *appointed time*. The Feasts are also called a *holy convocation*. The Hebrew word for convocation means *rehearsal*. Paul referred to this:

Let no one judge you in food or in drink, or regarding a festival or a new moon or Sabbaths, which are a shadow of things to come, but the substance is of Christ
Colossians 2: 16-17

It is more than interesting that God commanded that every Jewish male appear in Jerusalem at the Feast of Unleavened Bread; the Feast of Pentecost; and the Feast of Tabernacles (Exodus 23:14, Deuteronomy 16:6). God was not only calling Israel to a time of remembrance, but he was preparing Israel for the appearance of their long-awaited Messiah in the person of Jesus Christ. All males were to witness the crucifixion of Christ (Passover) in 30 AD which was the day before the Feast of Unleavened Bread Started at 6:00 PM). The *Paracletes (*Holy Spirit) fell on the Feast of Shavuot (Pentecost); All Jewish males (and their families) who will accept Christ as their savior will be required to participate in the last Feast of Tabernacles to celebrate Christ's victory at Armageddon (Zach 14:16-19). It is strange that after all that was prophesied in the Old Testament, and all that was written by the prophets of His ministry here on earth, that the Children of Israel failed to recognize or accept Christ as their long-awaited Messiah. We have shown how Christ satisfied and fulfilled each of the four spring festivals at exactly the appointed times; on exactly the appointed days; and exactly in type and substance.

Date	Feast or Event	Typology	Fulfillment
Nisan 10	**The Passover Lamb is Selected. "*Bring an unblemished Lamb into the house on Nisan 10, Four days before it is to be slain***	God commands Israel in Egypt To select a Passover Lamb for slaughter On Nisan 14.	**Jesus, the perfect Lamb of God, arrives in Bethany four days Before his crucifixion. He stood In the temple each day and was**

	And inspect it for spot or blemish" Ex.12:3-6		questioned by the Pharisees and Sadducees to find fault in him
Date	**Feast or Event**	**Exodus Typology**	**Fulfillment by Christ**
Nisan 15	First day of the Feast of Unleavened bread. A loaf of bread is baked from the Firstfruits of Barley (Old Testament Saints). It was prepared without leaven. It was offered to the Lord "*with fire*".	The Pharaoh let "*the Children of Israel go*" after his firstborn son was slain. The departure is in haste. The bread they took with them was unleavened	Christ lay in the grave the first day. He is the "*loaf without leaven*". He said "*I am the bread of life*". He is the "*first*" and only to live a sinless life under the law. John said he will "*baptize you with water and fire*"
Nisan 15-21	The Feast of Unleavened Bread lasted 7 days. Both the first and last day of the feast were "*high holy*" days... Sabbath days	The Children of Israel ate unleavened bread until God gave them "*manna*" from heaven.	Christ said "I am the Bread of Life". He was the true bread without leaven. He was sinless and blameless.
First Sunday in the Feast of Unleavened Bread	Feast of Firstfruits starts on this day...always a Sunday. The Feast lasts 50 days. Every day a	On this day the Children of Israel crossed over the "*Sea of Reeds*", and	Christ arose from the dead on this day. He was the "*Firstfruit*" unto God of all who will

	sheath of the emerging wheat crop is "*waved*" before the Lord. Also called the "Feast of Weeks".	was saved from death at the Pharaoh's hand. They emerged a new Nation under God.	someday also rise from the grave by believing upon His name.
Last Sunday of the Feast of Firstfruits	The Feast of Pentecost or Shavuot. "Penta" means fifty. Pentecost occurs 50 days after the first Sabbath (Saturday) in the Feast of Unleavened bread.	The Nation of Israel received the law from God at Mt. Sinai. The law was written on tablets of stone. The Levitical Priesthood was established. The High Priest was anointed to serve as the intercessor between man and God	On the Day of Pentecost Christ fulfilled his promise to leave with us an advocate: The Holy Spirit. On the day of Pentecost the Holy Spirit fell on the disciples and 5,000 people were saved. The new covenant based upon grace replaced the old covenant based upon the law. The new law of grace is written in the heart and not in stone

The first four Feasts of Israel have been satisfied both spiritually and physically. Their implications cannot be misunderstood by either Jew or Gentile if carefully studied.

The Fall Feasts of Israel

We have seen how Christ exactly fulfilled each of the four spring Feasts of Israel at his first coming. It is not difficult at all to believe that He will also fulfill each of the last three Feasts of Israel at his second coming. It remains to be seen exactly when this will be accomplished, but the prophetic fulfillment and relevance of each feast can be determined. The last three Feasts are partly concealed; and of course, hindsight in studying the first four Feasts is always better than foresight. Since all of the Feasts are Jewish in nature, we would be wise to examine what Jewish tradition has to say about the last three Feasts. In doing so, we will unveil a complete understanding of how we might expect this age of grace to come to an end. If Christ is going to satisfy the last three Feasts at his *Second Advent*, we can say with certainty that this will come to pass at the end of Daniel's last and 70th week. The events we will describe can only occur as Christ returns to the earth to reclaim it for His eternal Kingdom; set up His throne in Jerusalem; and purge all evil from the nations. The following diagram shows the relative timetable for these three final Feasts. They are:

(1) ***The Feast of Rosh Hashanah*** (*Feast of Trumpets*);
(2) ***The Feast of Yom Kippur*** (*Feast of Yom Teruah*) and
(3) ***The Feast of Tabernacles*** (*Feast of Booths*).

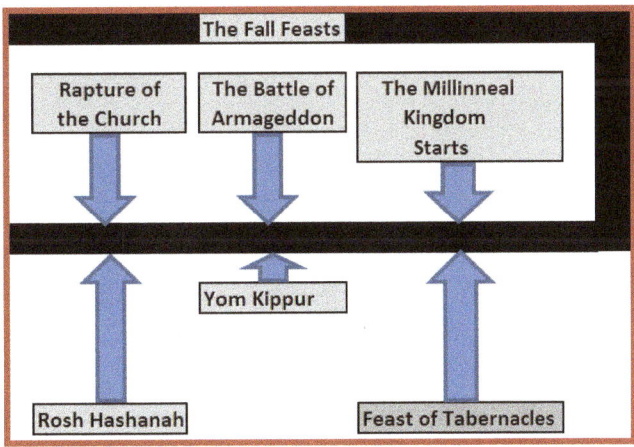

The three fall Feasts all occur in the Jewish month of *Tishri*. Tishri is the first month of the *Jewish Civil Calendar* and the seventh month of the Jewish religious calendar. All three Feasts will occur in a 22-day period of time in one of the Gregorian calendar months of September or October. Like the spring festivals, they are closely aligned and associated with the agricultural cycle. The month of *Nisan* brings forth the new crops of barley (Jews) and wheat (Gentiles). The month of Tishri ushers in the final harvest of wheat, corn, grapes and figs. Both the spring and fall festivals require rain to bring the precious fruit of the earth into full maturity.

Therefore, be patient, brethren, until the coming of the Lord. See how the farmer waits for the precious fruit of the earth, waiting patiently for it until it receives the early and the latter rain   James 5:7

The early rains fell on the newborn body of Christ on the day of Pentecost in 30 AD. We have been patiently waiting for the *latter rains* to fall when Christ returns for His second advent. As previously noted, the Feasts represent both historical and spiritual significance. Historically they represent significant events that occurred when God chose Moses to lead His people out of Egyptian bondage. Spiritually, each feast is a rehearsal or an appointment that God has made for Jesus Christ at His second advent.

There is an interesting correlation between the civil and the religious calendar. The civil calendar starts in September or October on Tishri 1. This is said to be the birthday of the creation of the world and the day on which Abraham was born. It is also when the wheat crop came to fullness and was harvested. The religious calendar begins in the month of March/April on Nisan 1. Nisan 1 is when the barley crop was coming into maturity and the wheat crop was starting to really grow. For those who have accepted the vicarious sacrifice of Jesus Christ on Nisan 14, the promise of resurrection from the dead and the gift of the Holy Spirit to every believer, the month of Nisan represents new beginnings in their spiritual relationship with Jesus Christ.

As we have already observed, there are almost 120 days between the Feast of *Pentecost* and the Feast of *Rosh Hashanah*. This is the long growing season for the precious crop of wheat. The wheat maturing and growing to the harvest is a shadow and type of the church age. The body of Christ is growing and one day God will declare that the harvest is near. We will not be surprised when the **war in the heavenlies** is seen (Revelation 12) and Satan is cast down to the earth. At that time, we will know that the tribulation period has begun. It is a fallacy that believers will not know when the end is approaching. There will be plenty of heavenly and earthly signs for those who are watching. It is certainly true that only God will know when the tribulation period will begin and on what calendar day the church age will end, but Paul in his first letter to the Thessalonians assured them that while the end will come suddenly, they were not to be unaware of what is about to happen. If this was true then, it is true now.

But concerning the times and the seasons, brethren, you have no need that I should write to you. For you yourselves know perfectly that the Day of the Lord so comes as a thief in the night. For when they say "peace and safety" then sudden destruction comes upon them, as labor pains upon a pregnant woman. And they shall not escape. But you, brethren, are not in darkness, so that this day should overtake you as a thief.   I Thessalonians 5:1-4

Notice that the apostle Paul is not denying that destruction and the Day of the Lord will come suddenly, but he emphatically and clearly assures them that they will not be surprised. Why would Paul assure them (and us) of this if it is not true? One thing should be pointed out which is highly relevant to our study. In the Jewish mind, the Feasts of Rosh Hashanah, Yom Kippur and Tabernacles are separate Feasts, but the Jews consider this time of year to form one season containing the three Feasts, just as the first four Feasts were generally called Passover.

The Feast of Trumpets (Feast of Rosh Hashanah)
The next feast of Israel that Christ is appointed to fulfill is commonly known as the *Feast of Trumpets*. What will this feast ultimately accomplish according to Jewish teaching? The answer might surprise most Christian readers. Sometime in the future, the Feast of Trumpets will be a time of great joy. The following events are taught to occur on the last Feast of Trumpets.

- The long-awaited Messiah of Israel will finally come on that day,
- The dead will be raised and given a body just like that of Adam and Eve before the fall,
- The earth will be restored to its former Edenic state,
- All men will be judged at this time,
- The Wedding Feast of the Messiah will take place,
- God's covenant with Israel concerning inheriting the land of promise will finally come to pass.

According to Jewish tradition, this *final Feast of Trumpets* will be initiated by the blast of a *shofar*. The *shofar* is not a normal horn, but is said to have been reserved for this special occasion since the *binding of Isaac*. Recall that God commanded Abraham to sacrifice his only son of promise, Isaac. As Abraham raised his knife to kill his son, God stayed his hand and delivered a ram as the substitute sacrifice. The ram was to be burned completely as a *burnt offering*. The only thing left was the two ram's horns. The *first horn* was said to have been blown on Mt. Sinai when the law was given; the *second horn* is reserved for the *last trump* at the last Feast of Rosh Hashanah (Trumpets). A special season which includes the Feast of Trumpets is called *Teshuvah*. It begins on the first day of the month of *Elul*, which immediately precedes the month of *Tishri*. Teshuvah lasts 40 days, and ends on the

Feast of Yom *Kippur* (Tishri 10). The Feast of Trumpets starts 30 days into the season of *Teshuvah* on Tishri 1. It is relevant that every morning during the month of Elul, a trumpet is sounded to warn all the people that the time has come to repent of their sins and return to God. Ask any orthodox Jew what the *last trump* means in relation to the ancient Feasts of Israel and the period of Teshuvah, and he will immediately respond the last trump is the *shofar*, which will be blown at the last Feast of Rosh Hashanah. *On the last Feast of Trumpets,* it is taught that there are several books which will be opened. The first is the *Book of Remembrance.*

Then they that fear the Lord spoke often to one another: and the Lord hearkened, and heard it, and a Book of Remembrance was written before him for them that feared the Lord, and that thought upon his name   Malachi 3:16

The second is actually *three sets of books*. Those who have committed to God and turned to righteousness are written in the *Book of the Righteous* or the **Book of Life** for the coming year. All other people living and dead are then divided into two groups. The first group is written into a book called the *Book of Rashim*, or the *Book of the Totally Wicked*. These are those who have totally rejected God and would not turn away from unrighteousness. The third or *last book* contains the names of those still alive who are not yet judged to be totally wicked, but have not yet fully repented and returned to God. Those people will have *ten more days* before their fate is sealed. These 10 days are called the *Days of Awe* and are the days between Nisan 1 and Nisan 10. The *Feast of Yom Kippur* occurs on only one day: Nisan 10. For this reason, the Feast of Yom Kippur is called the *Day of Judgment*. If these *gleanings* left in the *field* do not repent and turn away from sin by Tishri 10, their names will not be inscribed in the *Book of Life* for the coming year. If all of this sounds familiar to you, then it should. We have steadfastly maintained in this book that at the Feast of Trumpets, at the *last trump*, the rapture of the church will occur and the dead in Christ will rise to meet Christ in the air. These saints will receive their new, glorified, eternal bodies (Revelation 11:15-18). This will then initiate the *Marriage of the Lamb* (Revelation 19:7). The saints who are raptured and raised from the dead are those who have had their names inscribed in the *Lamb's Book of Life* (Revelation 21:27). The 10 days between the Feast of Trumpets and the Feast of Yom Kippur will be the last chance for all who remain after the rapture to escape eternal damnation. Those who reach the next feast, the *Feast of Yom Kippur*, without accepting Christ as their savior will be cast into the *bottomless pit* for 1000 years, and after the millennial Kingdom they will be raised and judged at the *Great White Throne Judgment*; they will then be cast into the *lake of burning fire* (Revelation 20:13). It is a sad thing, but failure of anyone to accept Jesus Christ as their personal Savior before they die is an irrevocable decision. There is no second chance.

There is yet another group of people to recognize: these are those who have missed the rapture and have accepted Christ as their Savior during the 10 days of repentance. This group is entirely hidden from Jewish teachings since they do not yet recognize Christ as Messiah and King. That group will pass into the millennial Kingdom with the 144,000 that were sealed in Revelation 7. They will have gone through the Wrath of God, which is the *Seven bowl judgments* poured out upon the earth between Nisan 1 and Nisan 10. Both our view of end-time events and the Jewish view of their salvation are perfectly aligned and consistent. The only difference is that the Jewish nation as a whole has been *blinded in part* until the scales are removed from their eyes and they can see. The Jewish nation as a whole is looKing for their messiah to arise and save them; their conquering King is called *Messiah Ben David*, not Jesus Christ.

But even if our gospel is veiled, it is veiled to those who are perishing. Whose minds the god of this age has blinded, who do not believe, lest the light of the gospel of the glory of Christ, who is the image of God should shine upon them II Corinthians 4: 3-4

Christ severely rebuked the church at Laodicea for believing in the world and not Him.

Because you say, I am rich, have become wealthy, and have need of nothing, and do not know that you are wretched, miserable, poor, blind and naked, I will spew (vomit) you out of my mouth Revelation 3: 17, 16

The Feast of Yom Kippur (Yom Teruah)

The Feast of Yom Kippur is on Tishri 10, which is also known as the *Feast of Atonement*. This day was a *holy convocation* and it was also a day of *fasting*. It was being observed when Nadab and Abihu, the two sons of Aaron, filled a censor with *profane fire* and used it to offer up incense in the Holy Place. Fire (coals) was not to be used at the Altar of Incense unless it came from the Brazen Altar. After their death, Aaron the high priest was told that he could not come before the Lord in the Holy of Holies without observing strict laws put down by God (Lev 16). The only day of the year that the high priest could come before God was on the *Day of Atonement*. On that day he would make a sacrifice for his sins, and then for the sins of the people. It was also on this day that two goats were chosen for a special offering to the Lord. One goat was for a sin offering unto the Lord, the other was to be led away into the wilderness and pushed over a high cliff outside of Jerusalem. This was called the *scapegoat*. The high priest would choose which goat would be the scapegoat by using the *Urim* and the *Thummin*. Once the scapegoat was chosen, a red scarlet cloth was tied around his horns, and the high priest would place his hands on the scapegoat, symbolically transferring the sins of the people to that goat. The scapegoat was then led away to a high cliff outside of the city and pushed to its death, symbolically representing the *removal of sin from the people*. The other goat was then sacrificed and his blood caught in a bowl. After cleansing himself again, the high priest would sprinkle the blood on the *Altar of Incense*, and then enter into the *Holy of Holies* behind the veil which separated the Holy Place from the Holy of Holies, where the Ark of the Covenant stood. The High Priest would come before the Ark and sprinkle the blood *seven times* on the *mercy seat*. The High Priest would then plead the sins of the people to God, who would come and dwell above the mercy seat in a cloud (Gaster). This is clearly a picture of Jesus Christ. He was *the scapegoat* who was led outside the city and put to death. Like the scapegoat, He took the sins of the world upon himself. *He who knew no sin became sin for us*. He was also the *sin offering* represented by the second goat. His precious blood was shed for us; it was sprinkled on everyone from Adam to the millennial Kingdom, and He sprinkled it Himself before the throne of God for the sins of all mankind. Jesus was *both* the sacrifice and the one who offered the sacrifice. He is now our High Priest who continuously intercedes for us and He sits on the right hand side of God the Father on His throne. At his sacrificial death, the veil in the temple which separated man from God was rent in two, from top to bottom. This represented that there was no longer a separation of the people from God, but now by the blood of Jesus Christ we can boldly go before the Throne of God in the presence of Jesus Christ who intercedes for us. He is both our *redeemer* and our *High Priest*. In one person at one cross, Christ was both the scapegoat for all our sins, and the blood offering to God. The writer of Hebrews spoke of the necessity for a blood sacrifice.

And almost all things are by the law purged with blood; and without shedding of blood is no remission   Hebrews 9:22

Now where remission of these is, there is no more offering for sin   Hebrews 10:18

The Feast of Yom Kippur terminates a 40-day period called *Teshuvah*. It begins on the first day of the 12th Jewish month of the civil calendar called *Elul*. The 30 days in Elul which precedes the Feast of Trumpets is a time when all Jews are to repent of their sins so that their name will be inscribed in the *Book of the Righteous*. As previously mentioned, the 10 days between the Feat of Trumpets on Tishri 1 and

Tishri 10 are known as the *Days of Repentance* or the *Days of Awe*. This 10-day period is the last chance that a person has to humble himself before God and repent of their sins for the previous year. On Yom Kippur, an individual's fate is sealed. At the last Feast of Yom Kippur, this will be a permanent and eternal fate. Jewish tradition teaches that at this time all persons will be held accountable for his/her sins. Perhaps of more significance to this study is the belief that on Yom Kippur the long-awaited Messiah of the Jews is expected to establish his earthly Kingdom in Jerusalem. Jewish tradition holds that the Feast of Trumpets will begin the 1000-year millennial Kingdom of Christ. We believe that they have missed this date by 10 days, and that the millennial Kingdom will start on Tishri 10 following the battle of Armageddon, but we will not be dogmatic about this point. It is crucial that the Jewish belief in their coming Messiah be completely understood. In the Jewish mind, there is much confusion concerning the Messiah which is mentioned many times in the Old Testament. In some passages, their Messiah is portrayed as being persecuted and scorned. In other passages He is predicted as a conquering King. To rationalize these conflicting accounts, it is taught that there would *be two messiahs* who were to appear. One is called the *Suffering Servant* or *Messiah Ben Joseph*. The other is seen as a *Conquering King* or *Messiah Ben David*. In Jewish eyes, Christ was the suffering servant. They are eagerly awaiting the appearance of the Conquering King. The arrival of Messiah Ben David will culminate in a great world battle for Jerusalem, in which the wicked will be vanquished and the righteous will inherit the land promised to them in the Abrahamic Covenant. Only after the 3.5 years of *tribulation* will Israel realize her error, the *scales will be removed from their eyes*, and they will know that Jesus Christ was both *Messiah Ben Joseph* and *Messiah Ben David*. He alone is worthy; He is the only son of the living God.

And so all Israel shall be saved: as it is written, there shall come out of Zion the Deliverer, and shall turn away ungodliness from Jacob   Romans 11:26

Jesus lamented of the error of the Jews when he spoke to His disciples on the Mount of Olives just before his crucifixion.

O Jerusalem, Jerusalem, thou that killed the prophets, and stoned them which are sent unto thee, how often would I have gathered thy children together, even as a hen gathers her chickens under her wings, and ye would not! Behold, your house is left unto you desolate. For I say unto you, Ye shall not see me henceforth, till ye shall say, Blessed is he that cometh in the name of the Lord.   Matthew 23:37-39

Hidden from their understanding is how *all Israel* will be *saved* as Christ returns to earth to fight the battle of Armageddon. It is spoken of by Zachariah.

In that day shall the LORD defend the inhabitants of Jerusalem; and he that is feeble among them at that day shall be as David; and the house of David shall be as God, as the angel of the LORD before them. And it shall come to pass in that day, that I will seek to destroy all the nations that come against Jerusalem. And I will pour upon the house of David, and upon the inhabitants of Jerusalem, the spirit of grace and of supplications: and they shall look upon me whom they have pierced, and they shall mourn for him, as one mourns for his only son, and shall be in bitterness for him, as one that is in bitterness for his firstborn. In that day shall there be a great mourning in Jerusalem, as the mourning of Hadadrimmon in the valley of Megiddo Zechariah 12:8-11

In that day there shall be a fountain opened to the house of David and to the inhabitants of Jerusalem for sin and for uncleanness. And it shall come to pass in that day, saith the LORD of hosts, that I will cut off the names of the idols out of the land, and they shall no more be remembered: and I will also cause the prophets and the unclean spirit to pass out of the land Zechariah 13:1-2

Behold, the day of the LORD cometh, and thy spoil shall be divided in the midst of thee. For I will gather all nations against Jerusalem to battle; and the city shall be taken, and the houses rifled, and the women ravished; and half of the city shall go forth into captivity, and the residue of the people shall not be cut off from the city. Then shall the LORD go forth, and fight against those nations, as when he fought in the day of battle. And his feet shall stand in that day upon the mount of Olives, which is before Jerusalem on the east, and the mount of Olives shall cleave in the midst thereof toward the east and toward the west, and there shall be a very great valley; and half of the mountain shall remove toward the north, and half of it toward the south. And ye shall flee to the valley of the mountains; for the valley of the mountains shall reach unto Azal: yea, ye shall flee, like as ye fled from before the earthquake in the days of Uzziah King of Judah: and the LORD my God shall come, and all the saints with thee. And it shall come to pass in that day, that the light shall not be clear, nor dark: But it shall be one day which shall be known to the LORD, not day, nor night: but it shall come to pass, that at evening time it shall be light. And it shall be in that day, that living waters shall go out from Jerusalem; half of them toward the former sea, and half of them toward the hinder sea: in summer and in winter shall it be. And the LORD shall be King over all the earth: in that day shall there be one LORD, and his name one. All the land shall be turned as a plain from Geba to Rimmon south of Jerusalem: and it shall be lifted up, and inhabited in her place, from Benjamin's gate unto the place of the first gate, unto the corner gate, and from the tower of Hananeel unto the King's winepresses. And men shall dwell in it, and there shall be no more utter destruction; but Jerusalem shall be safely inhabited.   Zechariah 14: 1-11

There seems to be no doubt about it: *That day* is the *Day of the Lord*, and the great battle being fought is the B*attle of Armageddon*. The reader is encouraged to do a short Bible study: Look up every reference to the Day of the Lord in the Bible, and without exception it always refers to a single day. Conversely, practically all of the *pre-tribulation* advocates refer to the *day of the lord* as being seven years long. Almost every classical advocate of a *pre-wrath* rapture make the *day of the Lord* 3.5 years long. *What has caused this incorrect interpretation?*

Without controversy, these incorrect interpretations have been caused by four critical mistakes: (1) Incorrectly assuming that the tribulation period was 7 years long (2) not recognizing that the *Wrath of God* is the pouring out of the 7 bowls following the sounding of the seventh trumpet (Rev 16:1), and not as the 6th seal is opened (3) failing to recognize that the 7 seals only provide an overview of the tribulation period, (4) failure to distinguish between *wrath* and *tribulation* and (5) refusing to recognize that the rapture of the church occurs at the seventh trump. We will develop each of these critical issues in later chapters. For now, let us continue our discussion of the three fall Feasts of Israel and their prophetic significance.

The Feast of Tabernacles
The Feast of Tabernacles is an 8-day feast. It occurs between Nisan 15-Nisan 22. King Solomon dedicated his new temple on the feast of Tabernacles. The temple of David was constructed for the Lord to come and *tabernacle* or dwell for a short time with man. It is the last of the three fall Feasts, and it follows the Feast of Yom Kippur. The historical significance of the feast is well understood. It commemorates the Exodus from Egypt, and the 40 years of wandering in the wilderness, in which the Hebrew nation dwelled in temporary tents called *booths*. The feast is sometimes called the *Feast of Booths*. The English equivalent of the Latin word for tabernacle is *hut*. A third name for the full eight-day feast is the *Feast of Ingathering* (Exodus 23:16). Harvest of the fall crops of wheat, figs and grapes are all completed at this time. The Feast of Tabernacles is one of the three annual Feasts at which every male Hebrew is commanded to attend in Jerusalem. The other two were the Feast of Passover and the Feast of Weeks (Exodus 23:17, 34:22, Deuteronomy 16:16). The feast is marked by celebration and praise to the Lord for both providing the crop just harvested, and for His provisions of quail, manna, and fresh water throughout the 40-year sojourn of the Exodus in the

wilderness. During the seven days between Nisan 15 and Nisan 21, the people live in temporary dwellings typically constructed of palm leaves and willow branches. This is a time of great celebration and introspection of God's goodness.

During the seven days beginning on Tishri 15, there were typically three daily acts of praise; (1) the people were to wave branches before the Lord …Leviticus 23 (2) there were daily sacrificial offerings…. Numbers 29 and, (3) the entire law was to be read in public gatherings. The entire 24 courses of priests were all put into service during this week. The last day of the feast is called *Shemini Atzeret,* referred to in the scriptures as simply the *eighth day of assembly* (Numbers 29:35). The term Shemini Atzaret is historically interpreted as *tarry or stay another day.* However, the Jewish emphasis on staying one more day as a request is not scripturally correct. The eighth day is ordained by God, and to stay is not an option but a command. The eighth day is primarily directed to the *Tefillat Geshem* or the *prayer for rain*. The months following Tishri are particularly critical to a successful planting season and a successful growing season. The *early rains* came during this time and nourished the emerging crops. According to Jewish tradition, God decides at the Feast of Tabernacles on the eighth day whether He will provide abundant rain or little rain in the coming months. The *latter rains* which occurred just before the month of Nisan enabled the crops to mature to fullness. The first and second coming of our Lord Jesus Christ was equated to the early and latter rains, which clearly reflected the Holy Spirit falling during his *first advent* and the pouring out of the Spirit of the Lord in the latter days at His *second advent.*

Be patient therefore, brethren, unto the coming of the Lord. Behold, the husbandman waits for the precious fruit of the earth, and hath long patience for it, until he receives the early and latter rain   James 5:7

And it shall come to pass afterward, that I will pour out my spirit upon all flesh; and your sons and your daughters shall prophesy, your old men shall dream dreams, your young men shall see visions. And also, upon the servants and upon the handmaids in those days will I pour out my spirit   Joel 2:28-29

The requirement for the Lord to be satisfied and produce an abundance of the early and latter rains dominated the temple services each day. Every morning in the temple the High Priest would go to the Pool of Siloam and fill a pitcher full of water. He would return to the temple among the people waving palm branches and reciting Isaiah 12:3: *With joy shall ye draw water out of the wells of salvation*. He would then enter the temple and pour the water out on the Altar of Sacrifice as all the people waved palm branches in the air as an offering to the Lord for His favor.

It was during this sacred ceremony on the last day of the feast that Christ arose, stood in front of all the people and shocked them all by loudly proclaiming: *If any man thirst let him come unto me, and drink. He that believeth on me, as the Scripture hath said, out of his belly shall flow rivers of living water*. Christ boldly spoke of when after his resurrection that the Holy Spirit would fall on all believers. This was the water that would continuously provide sustenance and never dry up.

A special season which ends on Yom Kippur is called *Teshuvah*. It begins on the first day of the month of *Elul*, which immediately precedes the month of *Tishri*. Teshuvah lasts 40 days, and ends on the Feast of Yom Kippur (Nisan 10). The Feast of Trumpets starts 30 days into the season of Teshuvah. It is relevant that every morning during the month of Elul, a trumpet is sounded to warn all the people that the time has come to repent of their sins and return to God. The first day of the feast (Tishri 15) and the last day of the feast (Tishri 22) are both *High Sabbaths*. There could be no work done on these days, and travel was limited to a Sabbath-day's journey. The cool evenings during this time were spent in a festive celebration. Every night there were torches lit everywhere to provide light. Dancing, rejoicing and banquets were enjoyed every evening into the wee hours of the morning. It was a time of pure joy. Tradition has it that no celebration in all of ancient Israel could compare to that which took place during the Feast of Tabernacles, and no single day could compare to the last day. The rabbis wrote: *He that hath not beheld the joy of this celebration had never experienced real joy in his life* (Joseph Good).

Jesus was undoubtedly referring to this joy when He spoke of the light that He can bring to all people who believe upon His name.

Then spoke Jesus again unto them, saying, I am the light of the world: he that follows me shall not walk in darkness, but shall have the light of life   John 8:12

A detailed study of the Feast of Tabernacles is both an enlightening and rewarding study. There are many shadows and types of Jesus Christ in this eight-day feast. The Feast of Tabernacles has significant application to the second coming of Jesus Christ and His initiation of the millennial Kingdom. After His second advent and the battle of Armageddon, the 144,000 Hebrews who have been sealed to enter the millennial Kingdom; the remnant who have survived the Seven bowl judgments; survivors of the sheep and goat judgment; the Bride of Christ and all glorified believers will rest at a great Feast of Tabernacles. It is also interesting that of all the Seven Feasts, only the Feast of Tabernacles is mentioned as continuing over the next 1000 years.

And it shall come to pass, that every one that is left of all the nations which came against Jerusalem shall even go up from year to year to worship the King, the LORD of hosts, and to keep the Feast of tabernacles. And if the family of Egypt go not up, and come not, that have no rain; there shall be the plague, wherewith the LORD will smite the heathen that come not up to keep the Feast of tabernacles. This shall be the punishment of Egypt, and the punishment of all nations that come not up to keep the Feast of tabernacles.   Zechariah 14: 16, 18-19

God will require that all nations attend the Feast of Tabernacles every year. Failure to do so will result in *no rain* and *a plague* to fall upon all those who do not obey His command.

Summary of the 7 Feasts of Israel
We have given a brief overview of the four spring Feasts, and the three fall Feasts of Israel. All seven Feasts are *rehearsals* for seven *appointments* that have been ordained since time began for our Lord Jesus Christ. The first four (spring) Feasts were fulfilled at the first advent of Christ, and the last three (fall) Feasts will be fulfilled at the rapture of the church and at the second advent of Christ. Collectively, all seven Feasts provide a *blueprint* for the work that Christ will accomplish. They also provide a blueprint of how the tribulation period will end. In particular, it is our uncompromising belief that at the last Feast of Trumpets, Christ will appear in the air and the *rapture* will occur, and that the battle of Armageddon will occur on the Feast of Yom Kippur.

Behold, I shew you a mystery; We shall not all sleep, but we shall all be changed, in a moment, in the twinkling of an eye, at the last trump: for the trumpet shall sound, and the dead shall be raised incorruptible, and we shall be changed. For this corruptible must put on incorruption, and this mortal must put on immortality. So, when this corruptible shall have put on incorruption, and this mortal shall have put on immortality, then shall be brought to pass the saying that is written, Death is swallowed up in victory. O death, where is thy sting? O grave, where is thy victory?   I Corinthians 15: 51-55

At the last Feast of Yom Kippur, Christ will return again, this time upon the earth and not in the sky. He will descend to the Mount of Olives to fight the battle of Armageddon.

Behold, the day of the LORD cometh, and thy spoil shall be divided in the midst of thee. For I will gather all nations against Jerusalem to battle; and the city shall be taken, and the houses rifled, and the women ravished; and half of the city shall go forth into captivity, and the residue of the people shall not be cut off from the city. Then shall the LORD go forth, and fight against those nations, as when he fought in the day of battle. And his feet shall stand in that day upon the mount of Olives, which is before Jerusalem on the east, and the mount of Olives shall cleave in the midst thereof toward the east and toward the west, and there shall be a very great valley; and half of the mountain shall remove toward the north, and half of it toward the south. And ye shall flee to the valley of the mountains; for the valley of the mountains shall reach unto Azal: yea, ye shall flee, like as ye fled from before the earthquake in the days of Uzziah King of Judah: and the LORD my God shall come, and all the saints with thee. And it shall come to pass in that day, that the light shall not be clear, nor dark: But it shall be one day which shall be known to the LORD, not day, nor night: but it shall come to pass, that at evening time it shall be light. And it shall be in that day, that living waters shall go out from Jerusalem; half of them toward the former sea, and half of them toward the hinder sea: in summer and in winter shall it be. And the LORD shall be King over all the earth: in that day shall there be one LORD, and his name one. All the land shall be turned as a plain from Geba to Rimmon south of Jerusalem: and it shall be lifted up, and inhabited in her place, from Benjamin's gate unto the place of the first gate, unto the corner gate, and from the tower of Hananeel unto the King's winepresses. And men shall dwell in it, and there shall be no more utter destruction; but Jerusalem shall be safely inhabited. And this shall be the plague wherewith the LORD will smite all the people that have fought against Jerusalem; Their flesh shall consume away while they stand upon their feet, and their eyes shall consume away in their holes, and their tongue shall consume away in their mouth   Zechariah 14: 1-12

And I saw heaven opened, and behold a white horse; and he that sat upon him was called Faithful and True, and in righteousness he doth judge and make war. His eyes were as a flame of fire, and on his head were many crowns; and he had a name written, that no man knew, but he himself. And he was clothed with a vesture dipped in blood: and his name is called The Word of God. And the armies which were in heaven followed him upon white horses, clothed in fine linen, white and clean. And out of his mouth goeth a sharp sword, that with it he should smite the nations: and he shall rule them with a rod of iron: and he treads the winepress of the fierceness and wrath of Almighty God. And he hath on his vesture and on his thigh a name written, KING OF KINGS, AND LORD OF LORDS
Revelation 19: 11-16

The Feast of Tabernacles will celebrate the second advent of Jesus Christ and His accomplished work. There will be great rejoicing and praise because: *the Kingdoms of this world will have become the Kingdoms of our Lord Jesus Christ.* This is the fulfillment of the angelic proclamation in Rev 11:15. There will be a great feast that will take place; the Marriage Supper of the Lamb. All believers will be at this Feast of Tabernacles. The Hebrews will inherit the land promised to them long ago; the saints will rule and reign with Christ; and the earth will return to an Edenic state. The 1000-year millennial Kingdom will be populated by the *earthly seed of Abraham*, and the saints who are the *starry seed of Abraham* will rule and reign with Christ for 1000 years. We are often asked the following question: *when will the rapture of the church occur?* To the amazement of everyone listening we reply; *On some future Feast of Trumpets, in the month of September or October.* To you the reader we urge you to *watch and wait, for the time is surely near.* It is hopeless and foolish to predict a date when our Lord Jesus Christ will return for His body, which is the church of all born again believers: But it is not foolish to determine the time or season.

The Seven Feasts of Israel

The Spring Feasts

Feast	Date	Prophetic Significance
Passover	Nisan 14	Redemption and Salvation. Christ was our perfect Passover lamb. The New Covenant replaces the Old Covenant
Unleavened Bread	Nisan 15-Nisan 21	Justification and Sanctification. Christ was without sin. He is the bread of life
FirstFruits	First Sunday of Unleavened Bread	Resurrection and life. Christ rose from the grave and conquered death
Weeks	Starts on Feast of Firstfruits and Lasts 49 days. 50th day is Pentecost	Sanctification and spiritual maturity. The Holy Spirit fell on the Day of Pentecost

The Fall Feasts

Feast	Date	Prophetic Significance
Trumpets	Tishri 1	Rapture of the Saints and Resurrection of the Dead. Wedding of the Lamb. Bema Seat Judgement
Yom Kippur	Tishri 10	Second Coming of Christ. Judgment of the Nations. Satan cast into Bottomless Pit for 1000 years. Antichrist and False Prophet cast into Lake of Fire
Tabernacles	Tishri 15- Tishri 21. Tishri 22 is a High Sabbath and a fast day	Beginning of 1000 year Millennial Kingdom. Tribulation Martyrs Raised. Judgement of the Nations

This concludes our study of the 7 Feasts of Israel and their prophetic significance.

Bibliography

Coulter, Fred R., The Appointed Times of Jesus the Messiah, York Publishing Company, PO Box 1038, Hollister, California, 95024-1038

Dake, Finis J., Dake's Annotated Reference Bible, Dake Bible Sales, P.O. Box 1050, Lawrenceville, Ga., 30246

Finegan, Jack, Handbook of Biblical Chronology, Hendrickson Publishing Company, Peabody, Ma.

Good, Joseph, Rosh HaShanah and the Messianic Kingdom to Come, Hatikva Ministries, PO Box 3125, Port Arthur, Texas 77643-0703

Horn H. S. and L. H. Wood, The Chronology of Ezra, TEACH Services, Inc., www.teachservices.com

Larkin, Clarence, Dispensational Truth, P.O. Box 334, Glenside, Pa., 1920

Logos apostolic Church of God and Bible College, Interlinear Greek and Hebrew Translation, Logos apostolic.org, United Kingdom, Logos apostolic.org

Nee, Watchman, Come Lord Jesus, Christian Fellowship Publishers, Inc., 11515 Allecingie Parkway, Richmond, Virginia 23235

Phillips, Don T., The Book of Revelation: *Mysteries Revealed*, 2nd Edition, Virtual Bookworm. com, PO Box 9949, College Station, Texas 7784.

Phillips, Don T., The Book of Ruth: *Historical and Prophetic Truths*, Virtual Bookworm. com, PO Box 9949, College Station, Texas 7784.

Phillips, Don T., Life After Death: *Mysteries Revealed*, Virtual Bookworm. com, PO Box 9949, College Station, Texas 7784.

Phillips, Don T., The Eternal Plan of God: *Dispensations, Covenant Promises, Salvation*, Virtual Bookworm. com, PO Box 9949, College Station, Texas 7784.

Phillips, Don T., The Birth and Death of Christ, Virtual Bookworm. com, PO Box 9949, College Station, Texas 7784.

Phillips, Don T., The Book of Exodus: *Historical and Prophetic Truths* Virtual Bookworm. com, PO Box 9949, College Station, Texas 7784.

Phillips, Don T., A Biblical Chronology from Adam to Christ, Virtual Bookworm. com, PO Box 9949, College Station, Texas 7784.

Phillips, Don T., Life After the Great Tribulation: *The Millennial Kingdom*
Virtual Bookworm. com, PO Box 9949, College Station, Texas 7784.

Phillips, Don T., The Last 50 Days of Jesus Christ
Virtual Bookworm. com, PO Box 9949, College Station, Texas 7784.

Phillips, Don T., The Daniel 70 Week Prophecy
Virtual Bookworm. com, PO Box 9949, College Station, Texas 7784.

Phillips, Don T., The Birth of Christ: A Forensic Analysis
Virtual Bookworm. com, PO Box 9949, College Station, Texas 7784.

Rosenthal, Matthew, The Pre-Wrath Rapture of the Church, Thomas Nelson Publishers, Nashville, Tennessee

Ryrie, Charles C., The Ryrie Study Bible, King James Version, Moody Press, Chicago

Salerno, Donald A., Revelation Unsealed, Virtual Bookworm.Com, P.O. Box 9949, College Station, Texas, 77842

Thiele, Edwin R., The Mysterious Numbers of the Hebrew Kings: Revised Edition, Kregel, Grand Rapids, Michigan

Thomas, Robert L., Revelation 1-7, An Exegetical Commentary, Moody Press, Chicago, Illinois

Thomas, Robert L., Revelation 8-22, An Exegetical Commentary, Moody Press, Chicago, Illinois

Van Kampen, Robert, The Sign, Crossway Books, 1300 Crescent Street, Wheaton, Illinois 60187

Walvoord, John F., The Millennial Kingdom, Academic Books, Zondervan Publishing Company, 1415 Lake Drive S.E., Grand Rapids, Michigan 49506

www.ingramcontent.com/pod-product-compliance
Lightning Source LLC
Chambersburg PA
CBHW061115170426
43198CB00026B/2991